GETTING STARTED WITH WORDPRESS®: DESIGN YOUR OWN BLOG OR WEBSITE

TODD KELSEY

Course Technology PTR
A part of Cengage Learning

COURSE TECHNOLOGY
CENGAGE Learning™

Australia • Brazil • Japan • Korea • Mexico • Singapore • Spain • United Kingdom • United States

Getting Started with WordPress®:
Design Your Own Blog or Website
Todd Kelsey

Publisher and General Manager,
Course Technology PTR: Stacy L. Hiquet

Associate Director of Marketing:
Sarah Panella

Manager of Editorial Services:
Heather Talbot

Marketing Manager: Mark Hughes

Acquisitions Editor: Heather Hurley

Project/Copy Editor: Karen A. Gill

Technical Reviewer: Mark Neal

Interior Layout Tech: MPS Limited,
a Macmillan Company

Cover Designer: Mike Tanamachi

Indexer: Larry Sweazy

Proofreader: Mike Beady

For product information and technology assistance, contact us at
Cengage Learning Customer & Sales Support, 1-800-354-9706.

For permission to use material from this text or product, submit all requests online at **www.cengage.com/permissions.** Further permissions questions can be emailed to **permissionrequest@cengage.com.**

WordPress is a registered trademark of the WordPress Foundation.

All other trademarks are the property of their respective owners.

All images © Cengage Learning unless otherwise noted.

Library of Congress Control Number: 2011924484

ISBN-13: 978-1-4354-6006-5

ISBN-10: 1-4354-6006-5

Course Technology, a part of Cengage Learning
20 Channel Center Street
Boston, MA 02210
USA

Cengage Learning is a leading provider of customized learning solutions with office locations around the globe, including Singapore, the United Kingdom, Australia, Mexico, Brazil, and Japan. Locate your local office at: **international.cengage.com/region.**

Cengage Learning products are represented in Canada by Nelson Education, Ltd.

For your lifelong learning solutions, visit **courseptr.com.**

Visit our corporate website at **cengage.com.**

Printed in the United States of America
1 2 3 4 5 6 7 13 12 11

To all my various college students and people I've helped with blogging, including Mom, Dr. Hein, Audrey, and students at WVU, including Juntae, Elisa, and others.

Acknowledgments

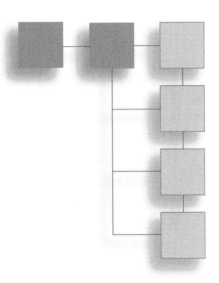

A special thanks to the following:

- All the people at Cengage Learning who have contributed to this book in some way, including but not limited to Stacy L. Hiquet, Sarah Panella, Heather Talbot, Mark Hughes, Mike Tanamachi, Larry Sweazy, and Mike Beady.

- Mark Neal, for helping to put together Chapter 15 and for tech editing this book.

- Heather Hurley, acquisitions editor, and Karen Gill, project editor, for putting up with my foolery.

- All the many volunteer programmers who make open source software possible, as well as the WordPress Foundation, for making a great product.

ABOUT THE AUTHOR

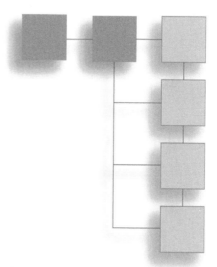

Todd Kelsey, Ph.D., is a Chicago-based tech professional, author, and educator. He has appeared on television as a featured expert and has authored books on topics such as social networking, Facebook advertising, and Google AdWords. He has taught at Chicago area institutions such as National Louis University, Westwood College, College of DuPage, and Wheaton College, and he has worked at companies such as McDonald's Corporation and United Airlines, in addition to nonprofit organizations such as La Leche League and the Cradle Foundation. His most recent research projects include starting a website about personal digital archaeology, with free material to help people capture their life stories and rescue digital artifacts (www.digitalarchaeology.org). He is also seeking collaborators to develop a nonprofit stock exchange (www.npoex.com). You can find him at www. toddkelsey.com.

Contents

Introduction x

PART I   **GETTING ACQUAINTED** **1**

Chapter 1   **Introduction** **3**
What the Heck Is Blogging? 3
Pros and Cons Compared to Facebook 8
WordPress Blogger 11
Hiring a Developer Versus Developing It Yourself 13
Conclusion 15

Chapter 2   **WordPress Alternatives: Starting with Blogger** **17**
Learning About Blogger 18
Starting a Gmail Account 21
Starting a Blogger Account 22
    Beginning to Blog 27
    Adding an Image 29
    Having a Bit of Fun 32
Conclusion 35

Chapter 3   **Starting a Free WordPress Blog** **37**
Deciding Between a Free and a Fee-Based WordPress Blog 37
Starting a WordPress Blog 41
    Making a Blog Public/Private 48
    Creating a Post 50

Creating a Post with an Image 52

Sharing on Facebook 56

Conclusion 58

Chapter 4   Working with Digital Images 59

Fine-Tuning Images While Uploading in WordPress 60

Using a Picture from Facebook in a Blog Post 67

Resizing Pictures with Picresize.com 70

Online Image Editing with Picnik.com 73

Managing Photos with Picasa 76

Renaming Pictures on Your Computer 77

Conclusion 80

PART II   LEARNING WORDPRESS 81

Chapter 5   Hosted WordPress: One-Click Installation 83

Starting a Hosting Account 84

Installing WordPress with QuickInstall 87

Extra: Redeeming AdWords Credit 93

Conclusion 100

**Chapter 6   Spam, Spam, Spam, Spam: Understanding Spam
and Security for WordPress 101**

The Bridge of Death: Ignore This Chapter and Be Sent
to the Gorge of Eternal Peril 102

Understanding Blog Comment Spam 103

Understanding Blog Security 104

Adjusting Comment/Spam Settings 104

Trying Out Akismet: Spam Killer 107

Updating WordPress So You Don't Lose Everything 111

Backing Up WordPress 112

Installing a Plugin: BackupWordPress 113

Exploring BlogBooker 118

Conclusion 121

Chapter 7   Easy Launch: Getting Your Blog Going 123

Tweaking a Theme 124

Setting Up the Basic Configuration 130

Making a Post 134

Conclusion 138

Chapter 8   Easy Content: Categories and SEO **141**

Categories 142

    Categorizing a Post 144

    Categorizing the Uncategorized Posts 146

SEO 148

    SEO for Writing Posts 153

    Getting Fancy Shmancy with the Code 156

Search-Engine-Friendly URLs 158

WordPress Versus Facebook Notes: SEO? 159

Conclusion 160

Chapter 9   Easy Insights: WordPress Stats and Google Analytics . . . **161**

WordPress.com Stats 161

Google Analytics 169

    Step 1, Option 1: Setting Up Google Analytics and
Getting a UID 171

    Step 1, Option 2: Returning to Google Analytics If It's
Not Your First Time 174

    Step 2: Bringing the Google Analytics Code Back
into WordPress 176

    Accessing Google Analytics 178

    Enabling the Dashboard Widget 180

Conclusion 183

Chapter 10   Easy Expansion: Themes and Pages **185**

Adding and Switching Themes 185

Adding and Accessing Pages 195

Conclusion 201

Chapter 11   Easy Expansion: Integrating Facebook and GTranslate . . **203**

Facebook Social Plugins 204

Changing Widget Settings 208

GTranslate 210

Share on Facebook 215

Conclusion 217

Chapter 12   Easy Expansion: More Plugins **219**

Browsing Plugins 220

Subscribing to an Email List 221

Exploring the Yet Another Related Posts Plugin 226

Adding Videos to Your Blog Posts 231
    Using Smart YouTube to Add Videos 231
    Embedding a Video Manually 235
Activating WP-reCAPTCHA 237
Perusing WP e-Commerce 241
Conclusion 244

PART III   SPECIAL TOPICS **245**

Chapter 13   Promoting on Social Media **247**
Copying a Link into Facebook 248
Importing a Blog into Your Personal Profile 248
Promoting Your Blog on a Facebook Page 249
Connecting a Blog to a Facebook Page 252
    Installing RSS Graffiti 256
    Accessing RSS Graffiti 264
    Importing Your Blog Posts into Your Personal Profile 265
    Going Mobile 265
Conclusion 265

Chapter 14   Promoting with Social Advertising **267**
Getting Over Intimidation 268
Creating a Facebook Ad 269
Accessing Ads 281
Making an Ad for a Facebook Page 283
Reviewing Performance 286
Starting a Revolution (or Helping One) 290
Learning More About Facebook Advertising 291
Investigating Other Kinds of Social Advertising 292
Conclusion 294

Chapter 15   A Few Sample Blogs **295**
Tour Stop #1: www.juntaedelane.com 295
Tour Stop #2: Digital Days 298
Tour Stop #3: Brotherhood of the Briar 303
Conclusion 307

Index **309**

INTRODUCTION

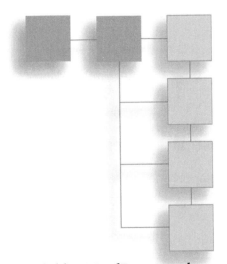

An open source content management system (CMS) like WordPress can be a great resource for anyone who would like to create a blog. It used to be that, to put content online, you had to manually assemble all the files and develop a fair amount of technical expertise; but a CMS can automate and significantly simplify many parts of the process.

The open source community surrounding WordPress has made it into a powerful and flexible product, ranging from the community of free blogs at www. wordpress.com, to the thousands of "hosted" blogs using WordPress software, supported by Internet hosting companies. The countless hours that volunteer programmers have put into developing plugins have resulted in an array of features that will meet just about any need.

A special note for trainers and teachers: the free version of WordPress can be a good place to start. If you cover the "hosted" version of WordPress, which requires a monthly hosting account, you could save money by creating multiple blogs under a single account for a class to share. For example, depending on the limitations of the hosting account, you could have www.classwebsite.com/blog1, www.classwebsite.com/blog2, and so on. With a company that supports quick installation as described in this book (such as hostgator.com), it's reasonably doable. Students who want to have their own hosting account could start their own. Also, in my experience, some students who are new to blogging have found WordPress to be intimidating, so Blogger can be a nice place for them to start.

WHAT YOU'LL FIND IN THIS BOOK

This book contains an easy-to-understand introduction to related concepts and a series of step-by-step examples that can help you learn to use WordPress to create and maintain a blog. This book starts with basic concepts, including looking at alternatives to WordPress, and gradually introduces various tasks. The coverage also includes using a "quick-install" web hosting account, which can greatly reduce the complexity of installing WordPress. (WordPress software is free, but you need a monthly Internet hosting account to run it on.)

This book is primarily about the "hosted" version of WordPress, which provides more flexibility and options for customization, but there is also discussion of the free version.

Chapter Overview:

Part I: Getting Acquainted

- Chapter 1, "Introduction," introduces the concept of blogging and looks at a few examples.

- Chapter 2, "WordPress Alternatives: Starting with Blogger," introduces Blogger, a free blogging tool that can be a nice place to start in learning how to blog.

- Chapter 3, "Starting a Free WordPress Blog," helps you start a free account at www.wordpress.com.

- Chapter 4, "Working with Digital Images," discusses several tools and techniques for working with digital images and pictures for blog posts.

Part II: Learning WordPress

- Chapter 5, "Hosted WordPress: One-Click Installation," helps you start a hosting account and take advantage of one-click WordPress installation, which can greatly simplify the process of getting a hosted WordPress blog going.

- Chapter 6, "Spam, Spam, Spam, Spam: Understanding Spam and Security for WordPress," is a crucial chapter that discusses how to manage/reduce the inevitable comment spam that you can get when you have a blog. It also offers simple but important techniques to help you prevent your blog from being hacked.

- Chapter 7, "Easy Launch: Getting Your Blog Going," includes a discussion of some basics for getting your blog started by adding content.

- Chapter 8, "Easy Content: Categories and SEO," introduces some techniques for building your blog, including organizing information with Categories to help people find your blog posts. This chapter also discusses SEO, otherwise known as search engine optimization, which can help your blog posts show up in search engines such as Google.

- Chapter 9, "Easy Insights: WordPress Stats and Google Analytics," talks about WordPress plugins, which add extra functions and features to a blog. Two plugins are featured, which can help you see how many visitors you've had and where they're coming from.

- Chapter 10, "Easy Expansion: Themes and Pages," helps you customize the look and feel of your blog with themes and explore the Pages feature in WordPress, which allows you to add conventional website pages to a blog.

- Chapter 11, "Easy Expansion: Integrating Facebook and GTranslate," discusses how you can add Facebook content to your blog to make it more social. It also covers the GTranslate plugin, which can make your blog available in different languages.

- Chapter 12, "Easy Expansion: More Plugins," explores additional plugins, including Subscribe, which enables people to subscribe to your blog by email; Related Posts, which includes links to additional posts that people might like to read; YouTube, which helps you include YouTube videos in posts; WP-reCAPTCHA, a nice method of reducing spam; and WP e-commerce, which can aid in your exploration of ecommerce on your blog.

Part III: Special Topics

- Chapter 13, "Promoting on Social Media," helps you explore how you can share your blog using social media tools like Facebook, to get more readership. This chapter also explains how you can make a Facebook page, as a method of establishing a "social media presence" for your blog.

- Chapter 14, "Promoting with Social Advertising," introduces you to methods of promoting a blog by running advertisements on Facebook to get more readers.

- Chapter 15, "A Few Sample Blogs," showcases a few sample blogs so you can see some of the things other people are doing.

WHO THIS BOOK IS FOR

This book is written with beginners in mind; no prior expertise is required, except some familiarity with how to browse the Internet and use a PC. For example, to build confidence and experience, an early chapter introduces the free version of WordPress, as well as Google Blogger, an alternative to WordPress that can be a good place to start learning about blogging.

Like any software, WordPress is not perfect, and its limitations are discussed openly, with suggestions especially suited for beginners on how to overcome them.

HOW THIS BOOK IS ORGANIZED

Part I, "Getting Acquainted," introduces you to blogging, including taking a look at Blogger, to build confidence. This Part also covers some tools and tips for working with digital images.

Part II, "Learning WordPress," is focused on starting a hosting account, installing WordPress with a time-saving one-click installation tool. It also discusses important basics such as security and configuration. You learn ways to add content to the site, including using various plugins that can add features and functions.

Part III, "Special Topics," introduces some techniques and concepts for promoting a blog once it is created, using social networks and social advertising. This Part also includes a few sample blogs, which some readers and classes might like to review first, to see some additional examples of the kinds of things people are doing.

At any point, you are welcome to visit the companion site for the book, www. wordpressprimer.net, to see more examples. You're also encouraged to email me at tekelsey@gmail.com if you would like to share a link to your blog or something you find helpful, to be posted on the companion site.

Alternatively, you can visit the companion Facebook page, where you can post links to your blog or elsewhere and participate in discussions with other people who are learning WordPress. See http://tinyurl.com/wpp-fb.

PUBLISHER'S COMPANION WEBSITE DOWNLOADS

You may download the companion website files from www.courseptr.com/ downloads. Please note that you will be redirected to the Cengage Learning site.

Part I

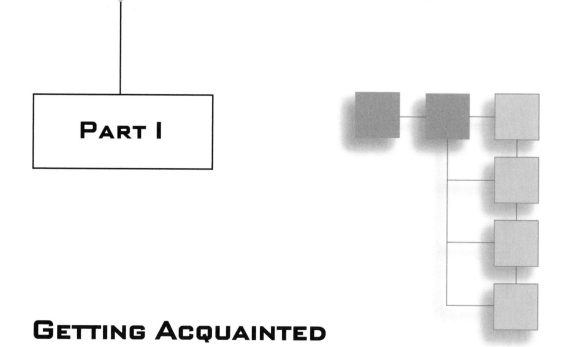

Getting Acquainted

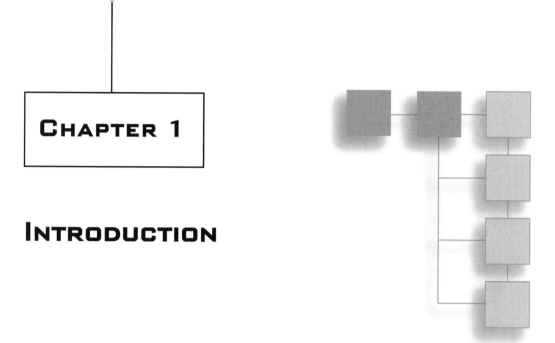

CHAPTER 1

INTRODUCTION

In This Chapter:

- What the Heck Is Blogging?
- Pros and Cons Compared to Facebook
- WordPress Blogger
- Hiring a Developer Versus Developing It Yourself

The purpose of this chapter is to introduce blogs and to help you get acquainted with some of the things you can do on a blog.

WHAT THE HECK IS BLOGGING?

A blog is basically like an online diary, or your own personal magazine. The word *blog* is both a noun and a verb. A blog is an online "place" where you can write things down and display pictures. It can be private, allowing only certain people access, or it can be public.

While blogs often are like journals or online magazine columns, it's important to mention that nowadays, people have pushed the WordPress platform so far that you can do just about *any* kind of website on WordPress, including using WordPress as a way to do ecommerce.

Blogging is an increasingly popular form of communication; there are millions of blogs out there, and millions of people are reading them. They cover just about any topic you can imagine. Some people write them for fun, and some as a way to make money.

You can "blog" by starting a blog and then writing things on it. Material you add to your blog is called a *post*.

For example, Figure 1.1 shows the first blog I created on WordPress.

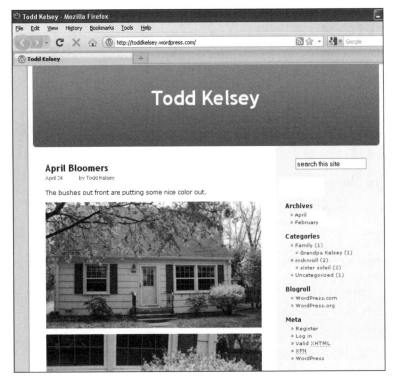

Figure 1.1
A simple WordPress blog.

On the right side of the page, you'll notice several things that are typical of blogs:

- **Archives.** This allows you to go back and look at posts historically (like looking at past magazine issues).
- **Categories.** This is kind of like a Table of Contents.
- **Blogroll.** This is peculiar to blogs; it's basically an area where you can tell people about other links you'd recommend they check out.
- **Meta.** These are functional links, such as logging in and logging out.

The design of my simple blog is . . . simple. I didn't really customize it because I was just trying out WordPress. WordPress *does* allow a high degree of customization, though.

Figure 1.2 is an example of a blog from a student in one of the classes I teach at West Virginia University's online program in integrated marketing communications. It's been customized with a special banner image and a variety of other features.

Figure 1.2
A WordPress blog with a customized look and feel.

Like my sample blog, the blog shown in Figure 1.2 is an example of a free WordPress blog. In a free WordPress blog, you can get an address like http://toddkelsey.wordpress.com or http://jillnadorlik.wordpress.com. If you want to get a custom address, such as www.mywebsitename.com, you'd need to pay for a monthly Internet hosting account.

One of the features about blogs is the way they're designed to facilitate conversation. One of the reasons people like blogs is because of the way they allow comments. For example, at the bottom of an article on Jill's blog, you can click the Leave a Comment link.

The meshing of social media and ecommerce perhaps is best illustrated by Payvment, whose app allows you to set up an online store within your Facebook page. Web designers, start your engines.

So what do you think 2011 will bring in regards to social media? Where's the next step?

Posted in Uncategorized | Leave a comment

When someone has left a comment on a blog, you can *read* the comments. You can set comments so that they appear automatically, or you can make them accessible with a link.

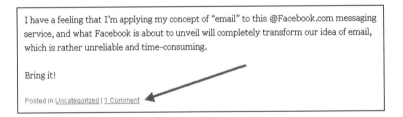

I have a feeling that I'm applying my concept of "email" to this @Facebook.com messaging service, and what Facebook is about to unveil will completely transform our idea of email, which is rather unreliable and time-consuming.

Bring it!

Posted in Uncategorized | 1 Comment

When you have a blog, you can control whether articles can be commented on. Some people like to blog without dealing with comments; others like to leave things open.

When someone comments, it's basically like filling out a form (see Figure 1.3).

When you post a comment, readers can be notified if someone else comments in relation to their comment.

Post Comment

☐ Notify me of follow-up comments via email
☐ Send me site updates

Leave a Reply

Your email address will not be published. Required fields are marked *

Name *

Todd Kelsey

Email *

tekelsey@gmail.com

Website

www.wordpressprimer.net

Comment

Hi Jill, I'm visiting your blog as an example for a book I'm writing.

You may use these HTML tags and attributes: `<a href="" title=""> <abbr title=""> <acronym title=""> <b> <blockquote cite=""> <cite> <code> <pre> <del datetime=""> <em> <i> <q cite=""> <strike> <strong>`

Post Comment

Figure 1.3
Commenting/Replies: the conversational part of blogging.

Blog posts can also include links at the bottom that make it easier to share, using email, Facebook, Twitter, or something else. You can also include advertising on your blog, which means that if enough people read your blog, you could actually make money.

You can also include a personal touch, perhaps through the design of your site, or through a section that includes something about you, the author.

About jnadorlik
A lover of communication, my background and education is in PR, Advertising, and now Integrated Marketing through my Masters program. I work by day in Marketing for a national brand in the hospitality industry and by night, am a student and social media consultant. In my spare time, I enjoy making soap, biking, and volunteering my skills to local non-profits.
View all posts by jnadorlik →

N o t e

Some blogs have multiple authors. They're very much like online magazines.

Blogs can become pretty influential; to see a list of the top 100 blogs, try visiting http://technorati.com/blogs/top100. The list can change from time to time, but there are typical leaders, as shown in Figure 1.4.

Figure 1.4
Some top blogs listed on Technorati.

PROS AND CONS COMPARED TO FACEBOOK

Facebook has become so popular that people are spending increasing amounts of time on it. One of the things you can do on Facebook that is very much like a blog is called a Facebook Note.

I like writing poems, and it's easy to just log on and compose a Note in Facebook (see Figure 1.5). All your Facebook friends can automatically see the Note in your newsfeed.

Figure 1.5
A Note in Facebook is similar to a blog post.

You can also make what's called a Facebook page, which is kind of like an official page for a business or organization. That page can have an address, like www.facebook.com/rgbgreen.

Then, on such a Facebook page, you could have Notes.

People could, in fact, access whatever you have to say through Notes on a Facebook page. When they click the Like button on your Facebook page, they will end up getting any of your future posts.

There's something nice about that, but the downside is that you can't customize a Facebook page as much as you can a blog.

My personal recommendation is to start out trying to make Notes on Facebook using your personal account so that your Facebook friends can see them. Then maybe even create a Facebook page. (See Chapter 13, "Promoting on Social Media.") This may be all you need.

But, chances are, if you're interested in WordPress, you want to have some customization and to go that one step further to get the word out, to express yourself, and so on.

So what I'd recommend at that point is to go ahead and make the WordPress blog, but then explore how you can import the blog into Facebook. That is, whenever you make a post on your blog, you can have it automatically import into Facebook so that all your Facebook friends see it (or so that it appears on your Facebook page, if you have one). That's the best of both worlds, and it's covered in Chapter 13.

Just to give you a little taste, see this article: www.facebook.com/help/?page=818.

You can also go to http://tinyurl.com/fbimportblog.

You'll see that you can Edit Import Settings for Facebook Notes. To do so, visit www.facebook.com/editnotes.php?import or http://tinyurl.com/fbblogimporter. The function doesn't work all the time, but it's worth trying.

So I have one of my blogs set so that it is automatically imported into Facebook.

So basically, whenever I write a poem, which is what I use my blog for, it also ends up on Facebook (see Figure 1.6).

But wait. Did you notice the address? This blog is at blogspot.com, not WordPress.

Well, that's because I use both Blogger (blogspot.com) and WordPress.

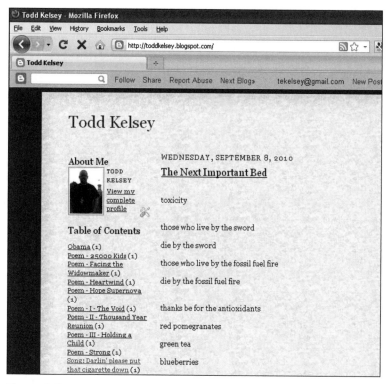

Figure 1.6
A blog that is also imported into Facebook.

WORDPRESS BLOGGER

Blogger, like WordPress, is a free blogging platform.

Blogger is convenient, because when you're signed into Gmail (http://mail. google.com—the best, easiest, most flexible email solution, in my opinion), it's a snap to sign into Blogger.

Blogger in general seems easier to use than WordPress, but it's not quite as customizable.

You can sort of make a Table of Contents if you tweak some things, but it does take some doing.

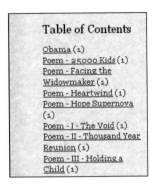

Table of Contents

Obama (1)
Poem - 25000 Kids (1)
Poem - Facing the
Widowmaker (1)
Poem - Heartwind (1)
Poem - Hope Supernova
(1)
Poem - I - The Void (1)
Poem - II - Thousand Year
Reunion (1)
Poem - III - Holding a
Child (1)

One thing Blogger doesn't include is the capability for advanced plugins like you have in WordPress (see Figure 1.7). Blogger has widgets, which can add a lot of functions, but there don't seem to be as many.

Figure 1.7
All in One SEO Pack is an option in WordPress to help a blog's posts become listed in search engines.

Plugins and widgets are basically extra pieces of software you can add to a blog if you want new features.

And if you need customized design and other advanced features, the paid version of WordPress (whereby you have a monthly Internet account at a place like Hostgator.com) has a lot of flexibility. That's where you begin to see a significant difference with Blogger, which isn't as customizable.

Still, Blogger is free, and free is always nice. Blogger also lets you have a custom website name, such as www.myblogname.com, that you can point at a free

Blogger blog, but with no monthly hosting fee. On WordPress, you have to pay a monthly hosting fee to get that capability.

So whether you should use Blogger or WordPress just kind of depends on what you want.

In the classes I teach, if a person wants to go all the way right into paid WordPress with a custom address and all the bells and whistles, that's fine.

But what I recommend, especially for beginners, and especially if you are looking to have fun and build confidence, is starting out simple and growing organically. That is, try the simple, free things first. Like maybe try making a Note on your Facebook account. Then try Blogger (see Chapter 2, "WordPress Alternatives: Starting with Blogger") because it's so easy. (With Blogger's fewer options, it is less likely to stress you out or be overwhelming.)

Then try the free version of WordPress (www.wordpress.com).

Then consider whether it's worth it to pay a monthly fee and take the time to customize and maintain a paid blog. Generally speaking, if your goal is ultimately to make money and sell things on your blog, you'll probably eventually want to have your own custom address and blog. But you could still benefit by starting simple.

HIRING A DEVELOPER VERSUS DEVELOPING IT YOURSELF

So if you fall into the group of wanting to go the whole way and have a fully customizable WordPress blog, one option is to do that all yourself; another option is to hire someone to help out a bit.

For example, my friend Audrey wanted to make a blog. She did research and decided that with the amount of customization she wanted to do, and because she really wanted to make money with her blog, she should get a custom blog. So she registered an address, got a monthly account, and hired a developer to get things going so that someone else could take care of the technical stuff and she could focus on her writing (see Figure 1.8).

Audrey also wanted to have a store. (See the Store link in Figure 1.8.) It turned out that the best solution for her was to sell merchandise through a CafePress

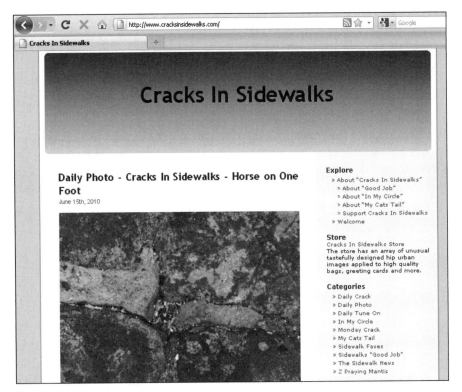

Figure 1.8
A WordPress blog on a monthly hosting account, with a custom website name.

store, because it allows uploading of art/pictures that it makes available on a variety of products (see Figure 1.9).

There's no right or wrong about hiring a developer or not; it just kind of depends on your resources and what you want to focus on. If you think you want to go as far as you can but are feeling a little intimidated by the technical side, maybe you could check into hiring someone. One resource might be a local college's computer science department.

Or you might feel okay about the technical side but be interested in hiring a designer to help you get the best look and feel. Feel free to reach out to some of my developer/designer friends:

www.theskyfloor.com: Alan and Joel

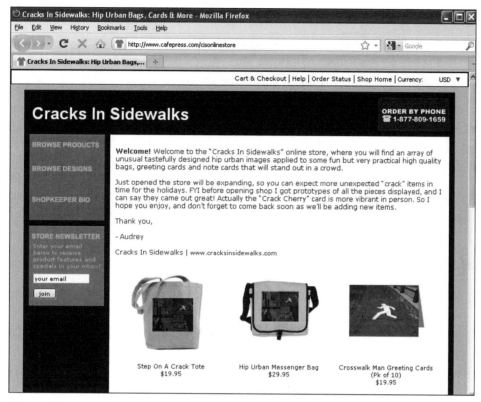

Figure 1.9
A web store from cafepress.com connected to a blog lets you upload your art and sell things to people.

www.cgadvertising.com: Alexandra

www.grafexguy.com: Jerry

But even if you see yourself working with a developer/designer, you could still benefit from trying a few things yourself, even on a free blog. In part, that will help you learn about the kinds of things you can do.

And you might even have *fun*. Woohoo!

CONCLUSION

Dear Reader,

Congratulations on making it through the first chapter!

A special congratulations to those who are feeling a mixture of excitement. . .and dread. Don't be afraid; together, we can explore the world of blogging. And if it helps at all, there are a number of people out there (fellow readers of this book, for example) who are going through the same thing you are.

You are welcome to email me at tekelsey@gmail.com and share your link to your blog on the companion site. Just visit www.wordpressprimer.net, and I can put your link up there. By the time this book comes out, you'll be able to see some links of what other people are doing.

Also, if you're on Facebook, you can visit the companion Facebook page, where you can participate in discussions with other people who are learning WordPress. See http://tinyurl.com/wpp-fb.

Regards,

Todd

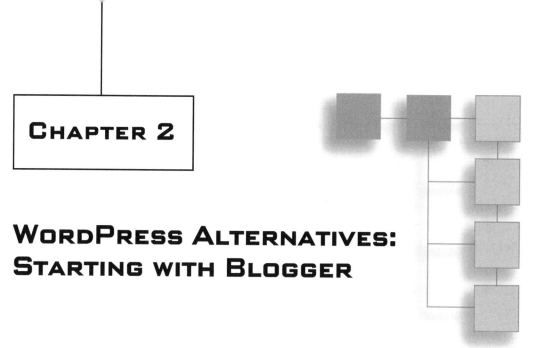

CHAPTER 2

WordPress Alternatives: Starting with Blogger

In This Chapter:

- Learning About Blogger
- Starting a Gmail Account
- Starting a Blogger Account

The purpose of this chapter is to take a look at Blogger, an alternative to WordPress. In classes I teach, I usually recommend that people try both, and especially for beginners, I recommend that they start by trying Blogger.

For some perspective, I'll share that at some point in the past, I had barely used any Google products; I was neither for nor against, and all I'd used was Google.com to search. I used Microsoft Outlook exclusively for email. Then I started having trouble finding old emails, and someone told me about the Google search plugin for Outlook. It worked really well. Then at some point I started trying Gmail. I thought it was a little weird at first, but again, it proved to be helpful. Over time I tried various free Google tools, like Google Documents (a free online alternative to Microsoft Word) and Blogger.

I think part of the reason I've ended up liking Blogger is because the blogs I've done have tended to be fairly simple, so there hasn't been a need for a lot of customization. I've been so busy that it's even been hard to find the *time* to blog, so having a tool that makes blogging as easy as possible has been nice. And I've appreciated that when I'm already logged in to Gmail, all I need to do is visit the blog and I will be automatically logged in. It's also easy to create and manage more than one blog. In addition, Blogger lets me take an address like http://2069. us and point it to a Blogger blog, so I can have a custom name without having to pay a monthly hosting fee.

I've also been happy with WordPress because of the level of customization and capability it offers, so I'm not *against* WordPress at all. I just think it can be helpful to consider alternatives, which is why I invite you to try Blogger.

Learning About Blogger

On the surface, Blogger blogs look like other blogs, based on how people have customized them. You might have an address like http://toddkelsey.blogspot. com (see Figure 2.1).

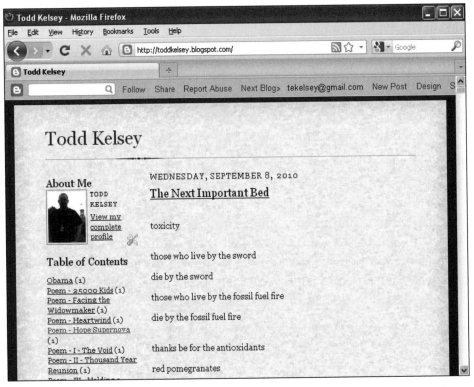

Figure 2.1
A basic example blog created on Blogger with some custom colors.

Or you might have an address like http://2069.us (see Figure 2.2), which is a custom website name that I'm pointing at in this other blog. (I chose to register a website name and point it, because it's a long-term, life-long blog about my goal of living to play at the 100th anniversary of Woodstock in 2069. It's also the story of fixing up a 1969 van and doing what it takes to fix up my own health so both the van and I can make it to the show.) You can go to a place like Register.com and look for what's available in terms of addresses. Or you can register at www.1and1.com. (Prices are reasonable.)

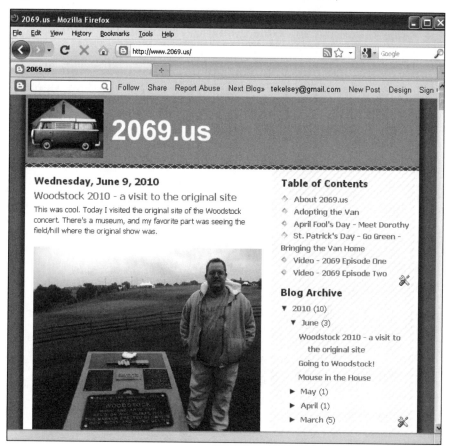

Figure 2.2
A Blogger blog, using a custom address that I registered at an outside company (www.1and1.com) and pointed to.

One of the nice features of Blogger is the way you can point a custom name at a blog without having to pay a monthly hosting fee.

As we see in the next image, at the top of Blogger blogs is a bar.

One of the things you can do is click Next Blog to browse through blogs.

When you're signed in, this bar is one of the ways you can work with your blog.

It's kind of a challenge to characterize the limitations and capabilities of Blogger versus WordPress in terms of design and customization. I have the sense that you can customize WordPress more, but you can do a fair amount with Blogger too, so depending on how much customization you need, the best thing is probably to try out both.

Here is an example of a fairly customized Blogger blog from a student (see Figure 2.3).

Figure 2.3
A Blogger blog with more customization in the look and feel.

STARTING A GMAIL ACCOUNT

You don't necessarily have to have a Gmail address to start a Blogger account, but I highly recommend it, based on how helpful I've found it to be. One thing you can do is have Gmail forward to another account if you still want to check your email at another address. But eventually you might end up using another of Gmail's features, which is to check other email addresses for you. For example, when I helped my parents try out Gmail, initially I set them up so that their Gmail account checked their AOL email address, and they've come to find Gmail very helpful.

To start a Gmail account, visit http://mail.google.com and click Create an Account.

While you're at it, if you haven't tried Firefox, I also highly recommend doing that (www.firefox.com).

If you'd like to try forwarding Gmail to another address, when you sign in, access Mail Settings (via the little Gear icon in the upper-right corner of the screen).

Then click the Forwarding and POP/IMAP link at the top of the Settings area, and click the Add a Forwarding Address button.

Gmail sends an email to the address you specify, and it has a code that you need to come back and enter into the field shown here. When you have the code, copy it over to this field and click Verify.

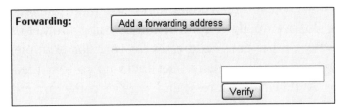

Then I suggest selecting Forward a Copy of Incoming Mail to your desired address and choosing Keep Gmail's Copy in the Inbox, which simply means that when you pass it on to your other email address, it leaves a copy of the email in your Gmail address. I think you'll find Gmail to be helpful.

When you're done, click Save Changes.

STARTING A BLOGGER ACCOUNT

To start a Blogger account, visit Blogger.com.

If you don't have a Gmail address, or if you are not signed into Gmail, the page looks something like this (see Figure 2.4).

If you have a Gmail address, you can use it to sign in by typing the email and password and clicking Sign In.

Technically, you can have a Google account using a non-Gmail address, but I don't recommend it. For example, if you have an email at Comcast.net or another Internet provider, what happens when your cable changes or the company changes?

Figure 2.4
Starting a Blogger account.

At the very least, you'll want to have a permanent email address at a place like Hotmail.com or mail.yahoo.com. If you want to use something like that, you can click on the Get Started link and use your non-Gmail address to create a Google account.

Otherwise, sign in with your Gmail address.

On the Sign Up page, enter a display name (usually your name, unless you want to be anonymous), click the I Accept check box, and click the orange Continue button (see Figure 2.5).

You are presented with a Dashboard, which is simply an area where you can adjust settings on your blog.

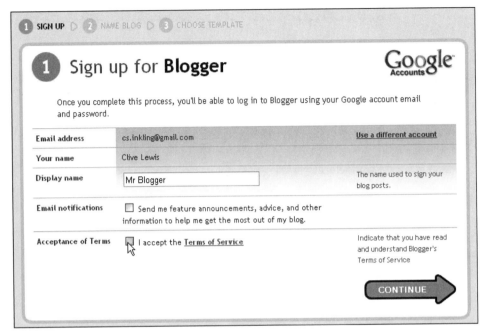

Figure 2.5
Basic choices for starting an account.

The first thing you'll want to do is click the Create Your Blog Now button.

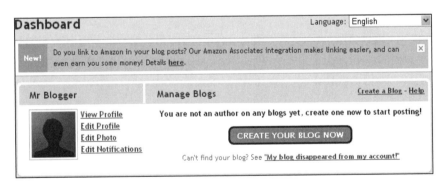

Then you have an opportunity to name your blog. The blog title can be whatever you want it to be.

The blog address, which is the link for your blog, depends on whether the name you want is available.

Just type in an address, and then click the Check Availability link.

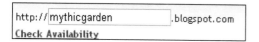

If the address is available, you get a message saying so.

If the address is not available, you have to try something else.

Tip

If your desired address is not available, try a poetic name or a combination of your favorite colors, or try dashes between the words you want. Because there are so many blogs out there, it can be nice to be able to use your own web address for a blog so you can be sure to get the address you want. But just keep trying, and don't worry. In the end, a blog is less about the address and more about what readers can find *at* the address.

When you're ready with the address, click Continue.

In step 2, you can have a bit of fun and choose a starter template; if you decide you don't like it, you can always change it later (see Figure 2.6).

Figure 2.6
Some of the templates available in Blogger.

Just click a template that you like to select it.

Then click Continue.

Next, click the Start Blogging button.

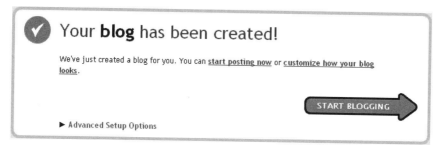

Beginning to Blog

The next screen that comes up is a Posting screen, with an area for a title for the blog post, and then a body area for the text of your post (see Figure 2.7).

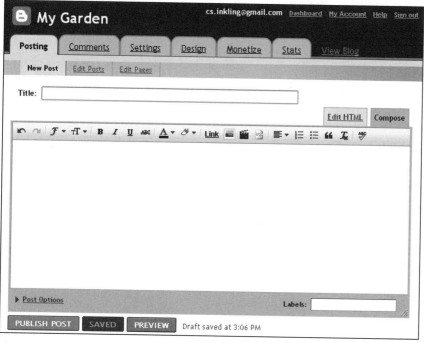

Figure 2.7
Creating a post.

Making a blog post is similar to writing an email.

In an email, you need a subject line, and then you write a message; sometimes you attach files, such as pictures.

To get started, just click in the Title area, type something in, and then click in the lower area and type something.

And then just click the Publish Post button.

Woohoo! You just made a blog post.

> **Your blog post published successfully!**
>
> **View Post** ▣
>
> Need to change it? Edit post | Create a new post

If you want to get fancy, right-click (Windows) or Ctrl-click (Mac) and choose Open Link in New Tab. This can be a nice technique so you can look at your blog in another tab and keep the Dashboard open in the current tab. If your browser doesn't have tabs, try downloading a recent version of Firefox (www.firefox.com).

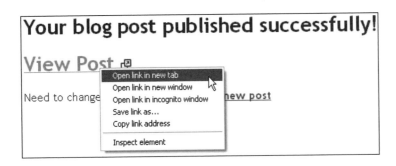

Voilà! The blog is shown in Figure 2.8.

Figure 2.8
The new Blogger blog.

Next, click on the New Post link in the upper-right corner of the blog when you're signed in so you can try making a post with an image.

Adding an Image

Now we'll have some fun by adding an image to a blog post. Visuals can make things interesting; it could be a digital picture you took or any other kind of image, such as from a place like www.publicdomainpictures.net.

If you'd like a test image, I've made the one I'm using below available at www.wordpressprimer.net/files.

To get started, type in a title and some text, and press the Enter key a few times to move the cursor down a line or two. Then click the Insert Image button.

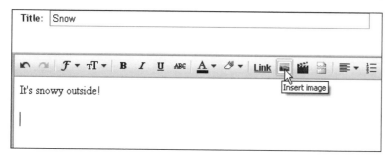

Note

If you see different buttons appear here, you might be using the old blog editor. To use the updated editor, log into Blogger, go under the Settings tab, scroll down to Select Post Editor, click the Updated Editor radio button, and click the Save Settings button.

Next, you're presented with the Add Images window. Click the Choose Files button, locate an image on your computer, and double-click on it (see Figure 2.9).

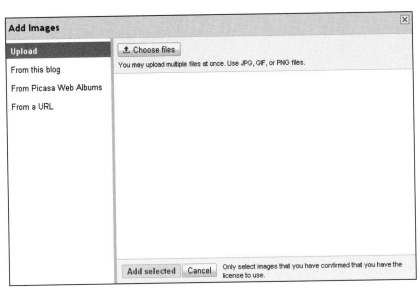

Figure 2.9
Adding an image.

After the image uploads, a thumbnail version will appear with a solid line around it to indicate that it is selected.

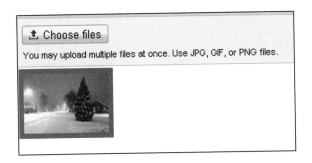

Next, click the Add Selected button.

Add selected

Then the image appears in your blog post, possibly in the center.

To play with the image position or size, just click on it. Try clicking on one of the links that appear beneath the image, such as Left (see Figure 2.10).

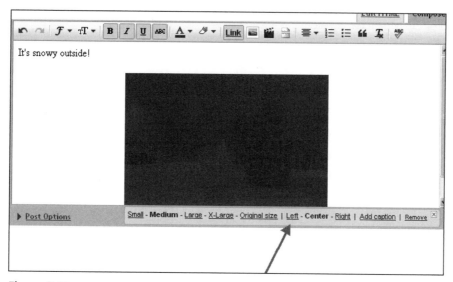

Figure 2.10
Making adjustments to an added image.

Clicking on the Left link should move the image to the left. You can also click on the size links, such as Small, Medium, and Large.

To hide the blue selection bar, click on the background of your post or on the little X in the upper-right corner of the blue selection bar (see Figure 2.11).

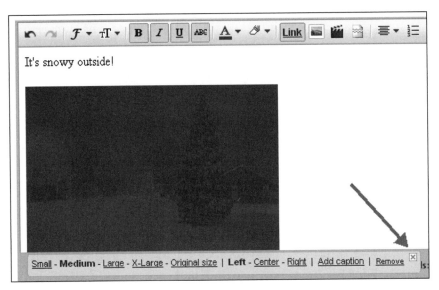

Figure 2.11
You can get rid of the pop-up bar by clicking the X.

Woohoo! The image appears as part of the post, and you can click the Publish Post button (see Figure 2.12).

And if all goes well, you'll see something like Figure 2.13.

Congratulations! You've just made a post!

Having a Bit of Fun

For a bit of extra fun, we'll look at how to share the post on Facebook. If you're not on Facebook, no problem; if you'd like to try it, visit www.facebook.com, or download a free copy of the sample edition of Social Networking Spaces at http://tinyurl.com/snspaces-sed by clicking the Download link. (There's an introductory chapter on Facebook.)

Figure 2.12
A blog post, ready for publishing.

Figure 2.13
The custom look and feel applied to the blog.

To share your new blog on Facebook, you'll want to become familiar with what the address is.

So if we look at the Internet browser, we'll see something like this when we make a post.

If I wanted to share a link to that post, I could click, drag, select, and copy the entire link.

If I wanted to be fancy, I could triple-click to select the post and then right-click to copy it.

Or if I wanted to share the general blog address, it would be the first part, like this:

mythicgarden.blogspot.com

Or

aboutrgb.blogspot.com

Then, strictly speaking, you could just share the links without putting www before them. In this situation, there's no need to put a www before the address, but you might want to put an http:// before it, so it might be this:

http://aboutrgb.blogspot.com

To have some fun, log into Facebook and look for something like this.

Then type in a few words, and paste or type your link. After that, click Share.

Woohoo! You've posted your blog to Facebook.

CONCLUSION

Dear Reader,

Congratulations on making it through this chapter.

You're now a blogger. You've blogged. You've engaged in bloggery. You've posted. Yeehaw!

If you like, feel free to visit www.wordpressprimer.net/blogs and view other readers' blogs. You can even share a link to your blog.

If you're on Facebook, you can visit the WordPress Primer Facebook page to post your blog and see links to other blogs. See www.facebook.com/pages/WordPress-Primer/186134644744074 or http://tinyurl.com/wpp-fb.

Regards,

Todd

CHAPTER 3

STARTING A FREE WORDPRESS BLOG

In This Chapter:

- Deciding Between a Free and a Fee-Based WordPress Blog
- Starting a WordPress Blog

The purpose of this chapter is to get you started with making a free WordPress blog so you can learn how it works; later on you can decide whether you would rather have a fee-based blog.

Let's get started!

DECIDING BETWEEN A FREE AND A FEE-BASED WORDPRESS BLOG

You start a free WordPress blog by visiting and registering at www.wordpress. com.

In a free WordPress blog, you get an address "at" WordPress, like http:// toddkelsey.wordpress.com.

In a fee-based WordPress blog, you can use a custom website name.

For example, Figure 3.1 is an example of a highly polished WordPress blog from a student, with a custom address.

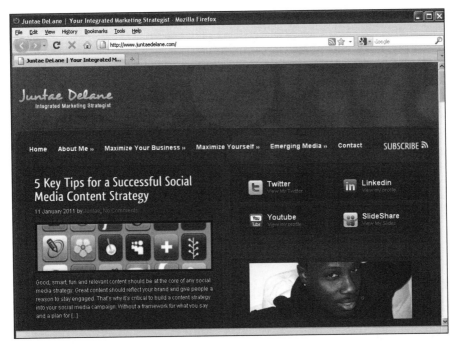

Figure 3.1
A WordPress blog with a polished design.

A fee-based WordPress blog can be hosted at any Internet hosting company that supports WordPress. The general process is that you start an account, register a website name (such as www.myblogwebsite.com), and then use a one-click installation to install WordPress for your website. We'll take a look at that process starting in Chapter 5, "Hosted WordPress: One-Click Installation."

Note

If you already have a website name and aren't using it yet, and if your hosting company doesn't support WordPress with one-click installation, you can always point your website name at a place that does. In that case, you would continue to pay the yearly fee for the cost of maintaining the registration of the website name (maybe $12 per year) at the original company (or you could transfer the name), and then you would pay a monthly fee for hosting at the new company. See Chapter 5.

There's one other configuration of WordPress that's interesting: WordPress Multi-User. I'm not sure if anyone has this available on a one-click installation; it probably requires the services of a developer.

To clarify, you can have multiple people sign in and work on a single blog; many people do that. What WordPress Multi-User basically does is give you your own "WordPress.com," in effect. It allows companies or organizations to have custom blogs "at" their website name.

For example, I hired a friend, Seth Woodworth, to try an experiment for the Sunflower Club using WordPress Multi-User, because I thought it would be nice to let people have themed blogs "at" SunflowerClub.net.

So a few people in the Sunflower Club tried it out. There was an http://walter.sunflowerclub.net, an http://todd.sunflowerclub.net, and more. See Figure 3.2 and Figure 3.3.

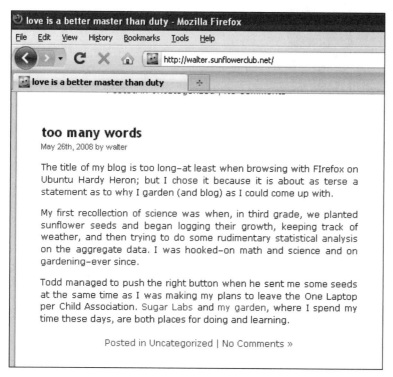

Figure 3.2
An example of how WordPress Multi-User can allow you to have multiple blogs at your own website, such as john.mywebsite.com and jane.mywebsite.com.

Figure 3.3
Another blog, at the same website, managed by WordPress Multi-User.

Since then, it seemed like it might just be easier to invite people to make blogs or post pictures wherever they wanted, such as on their Facebook accounts, because of convenience. So there didn't turn out to be a need for WordPress Multi-User.

WordPress Multi-User might be best for a company or organization that wants to have a community of blogs at a single website address. Then again, when you own a website name, depending on your hosting company, you can manually create addresses like http://todd.sunflowerclub.net or http://walter. sunflowerclub.net, and you can point these at individual blogs. It just depends on what your goals are.

STARTING A WORDPRESS BLOG

To start a WordPress blog (or to become pleasantly distracted by reading other blogs), just visit www.wordpress.com and click Sign Up Now (see Figure 3.4).

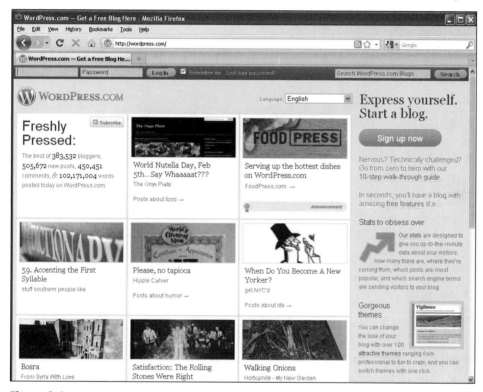

Figure 3.4
WordPress.com allows you to start a blog or browse others' blogs.

Notice the link for a nice 10-step guide that WordPress has, available at http://learn.wordpress.com (see Figure 3.5).

After clicking Sign Up Now, choose your username. This could be your name or anything else you want it to be, as long as someone else isn't already using it.

Get your own WordPress.com account in seconds

Fill out this one-step form and you'll be blogging seconds later!

Blog Address

[   ] .wordpress.com

Want your own domain?

Choose a wordpress.com address or get your own URL with a custom domain name. (?)

Sign up for just a username.

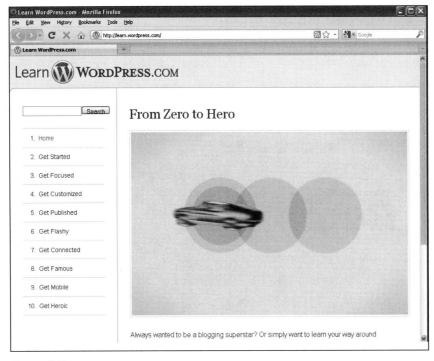

Figure 3.5
Learn.WordPress.com.

Keep trying names until you get a little green checkmark on the right side.

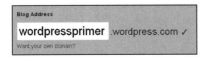

WordPress now has the integrated ability to offer you a custom WordPress website name. If you click on the Want Your Own Domain link, you get the following box.

(To get back to the other screen, you can click No Thanks.)

Note that using a website name (domain name) with a free WordPress blog still entails a limited blog. That means there's no monthly fee, but you have some customization limitations. For example, you can't use any plugin you like. There are some built-in plugins on WordPress.com, but you can't use whatever plugin you want; for some people, this is a limitation.

My recommendation is to start out with a free WordPress blog and use a free username, like myblogrocks.wordpress.com. This way you can see what the free version's capabilities and limitations are. If this version does everything you want but you would like to have a custom name, like www.igrowbananas.com, come back and click the Want Your Own Domain link.

If you look through the rest of the book and at plugins, and it feels like you really do want a "full" hosted WordPress blog, you can start an account at a place like HostGator.com and go for the full package.

Here is what WordPress.com has to say about plugins on the free version of WordPress (http://en.support.wordpress.com/plugins/).

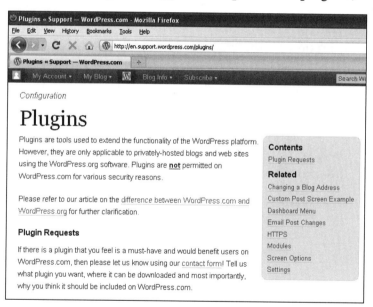

After you choose your blog address, WordPress may prefill a username. To keep things simple, I recommend keeping the username the same as the blog address, but you can certainly change it if you like.

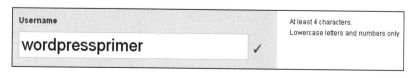

Then you need to come up with a password.

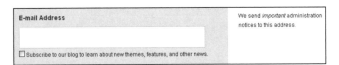

To keep the password secure and to keep track of your account information, I recommend going elsewhere on your computer, creating a new folder, calling it Accounts, and then starting a text document with account information for each online account. For WordPress, I'd keep a record of your username and the address of the blog; then for a password, I'd type in some random characters, like this:

    ss642$s@

This is much more secure than `mypassword` or your birth date. I do recommend using the feature in Firefox and other browsers to store passwords to keep things easy, but sometimes browsers crash, so it's good to have a record of your username and password somewhere.

And if you really want to keep things secure, look on Amazon.com for a click-free backup drive; it's easy to use, and it's a great way to back up your computer's information. Or if you are on a Mac and can afford it, the Time Machine is a great wireless backup device.

Enter your password, enter it again in the Confirm box, and then enter your email address.

If you're a new blogger, you might even want to click the Subscribe check box.

Then click the Sign Up button.

Hee hee. I like the way WordPress refers to its terms of service: "fascinating."

Next, WordPress sends you an activation email. In the body of the email, click on the link to complete registration.

Check Your E-mail to Complete Registration

An e-mail has been sent to **cftwgreen@gmail.com** to activate your account. Check your inbox and click the link in the message. It should arrive within 30 minutes. If you do not activate your account within two days, you will have to sign up again.

In the meantime, you can fill in your profile. Then click Save Profile.

Update Your Profile!

If you haven't got your activation e-mail why not update your profile while you wait?

First Name:

Last Name:

About Yourself:

Save Profile →

Then when you click on the activation link in the email, you should get something like this:

Your account is now active!

Username:	Password:
wordpressprimer	********************************

Your account is now active. View your site or Login

If you like, you can click on the View Your Site link.

Congratulations! You've created your blog. It prefills a blog post for you (see Figure 3.6).

The blog address is based on your username (such as http://wordpressprimer.wordpress.com).

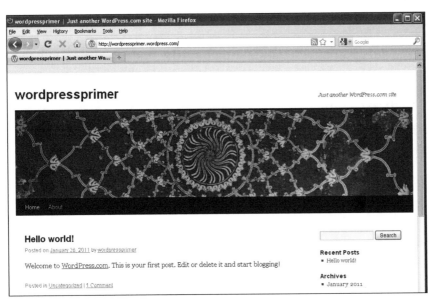

Figure 3.6
A sample newly started WordPress blog.

At some point you need to log in. On your blog, you can always scroll down; on the right side, click on the Log In link.

Then you can enter your username and password. After that, click Remember Me, and click the Log In button.

Note

If you're on Firefox, keep your eyes open for the Remember Password bar toward the top of the browser window.

WordPress may pop up a helpful message when you log in for the first time.

When you want to close the window, click the X in the upper-left corner. (It may appear differently depending on your browser and operating system.)

What the note is referring to is the fact that you have a Dashboard link, which is separate from your main blog address.

So when you notice something like this in your browser window, I'd recommend bookmarking it (and copying it into your username password document if you made one of those).

This is the Dashboard link, also known as the admin link. Strictly speaking, you could always just go to the main address for your blog, scroll down, and click the Log In link, but bookmarking the direct link to the Dashboard might be helpful.

The Dashboard is the behind-the-scenes screen where you adjust settings and make posts.

Then, by comparison, your main blog address would look something like this.

This is the link you would put on your business cards or on Facebook.

When you log into the blog, you get the Dashboard, where all the magic happens (see Figure 3.7).

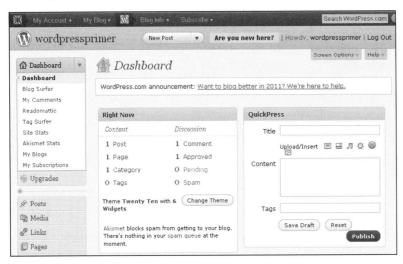

Figure 3.7
Dashboard: behind the scenes in a WordPress blog.

Don't worry if you feel overwhelmed by all the links and possibilities; you're not alone. We'll take a look at some simple things you can try to gain confidence and to get used to the various options. The most important thing is to have fun!

Making a Blog Public/Private

While we're looking at the Dashboard, it's helpful to consider that you can have a private or public blog. (You can also have more than one blog.) For example, my mom wanted to make an electronic version of some memories she had written down so that my brother and I could access them easily, so she made a private blog that only the family can see. WordPress might be a way to make a private family site, for example.

If you want to make a private blog (you can always change it back and forth), scroll down in the Dashboard and click the Settings link on the left.

Then click the Privacy link.

To make the blog private, just click the I Would Like My Blog to Be Private radio button, and then click the Save Changes button.

Then you are given the opportunity to add up to 35 users. I believe that to access the blog, people need to sign up on WordPress.com. (There is an option to create a username only if they don't want to make a blog. You could create the account for them and then tell them an activation email is on the way.)

You can always come back and change things later.

When you're done, click Save Changes.

And if you're following along learning and you've just made your blog private but you really want a public blog, remember to make it public!

Then, if you feel like you're in Oz and you want to get back to Kansas, you can always click on the Dashboard link to get back home.

Creating a Post

Okie dokie. Now we'll have some fun and create a post!

To create a post, search for the New Post button on the WordPress Dashboard, and click it.

The first thing you do when you're creating a blog post is to add a title, like you would in an email subject line. Just click in the white area underneath Add New Post and type something.

![Add New Post]

Then click in the text area down below, and type something there.

N o t e

The little icons above the text area are for formatting. For example, if you select the text and click the B icon, WordPress makes your text bold. It works just like a word processing program.

Look over on the right side of the screen for the Publish panel. Don't worry about all the options; just click the Publish button.

If you're feeling up to it, you might like to try getting into the habit of clicking on anything and everything. Think of it as an adventure. If you'd like the chance to review or add to the content before publishing, though, you're not alone. Lots of bloggers write drafts and keep tweaking them before they publish them.

Woohoo! You published a post. Now you can click on the View Post link.

Or, if you want to be fancy, you can right-click (Windows) or Ctrl-click (Mac) and choose something like Open Link in New Tab, so that your public blog is in one tab, and your Dashboard stays right where it is. There's no right or wrong way of doing things here. It just depends on how you like to work with windows.

There, on your blog, is your post. Congrats!

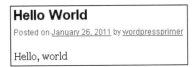

Creating a Post with an Image

Next, we'll have some fun adding an image to a post.

Accessing Your Dashboard

If you're not sure how to get to your Dashboard, remember that there's an admin link that will be something like this:

http://wordpressprimer.wordpress.com/wp-admin

Or you can go to the main blog link, which will be something like this:

http://wordpressprimer.wordpress.com

On the main blog, when you are logged in, you can click the Site Admin link (see Figure 3.8) to get to your Dashboard. (If you're not logged in, you can click on the Log In link.)

When you're logged in, you can get around easily by rolling your mouse pointer over the My Blog link at the top, and then clicking on Dashboard.

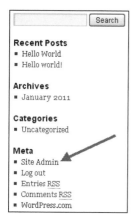

Figure 3.8
The Site Admin link is a way to get to the Dashboard.

Using this technique, you can jump back and forth in the same window. Look, ma, no tabs!

Making a Post with an Image

So making a post with an image is the same as any other post; start by clicking the New Post button.

Enter a title in the top-white bar, click below, and enter some text. Press the Enter key a few times so the cursor goes down lower, and then click the Add Image icon (as shown by the arrow).

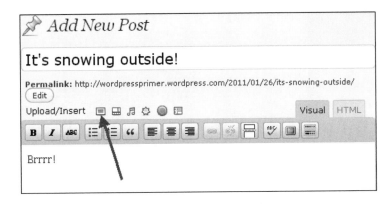

What you need to do is to find an image on your computer to upload. Perhaps it's a digital picture from your camera or an image you downloaded from www.publicdomainpictures.net.

If you would like a test image, I've made the one I'm using below available at www.wordpressprimer.net/files.

Next, in the Add Media Files window, click the Select Files button.

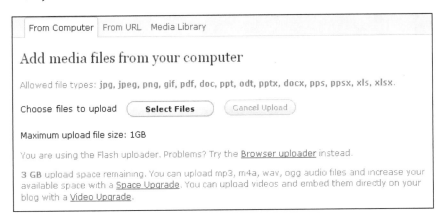

Locate a picture file on your computer, and double-click on it. It uploads, and then you end up with a window like this next one (see Figure 3.9). Don't worry about all the options in this window; just click the Insert into Post button.

Then hopefully you'll see something like Figure 3.10.

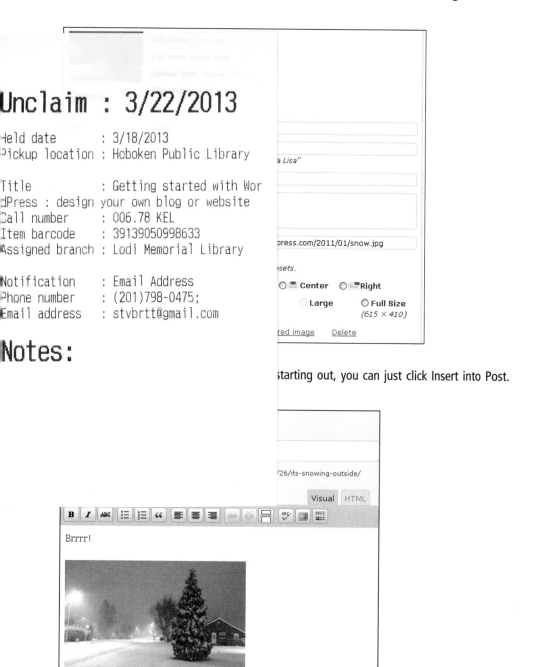

starting out, you can just click Insert into Post.

Figure 3.10
A post with an image inserted.

Then you can click the Publish button on the right side of the Dashboard screen.

To see the post, click View Post.

Woohoo! You've made a blog post with a picture.

Sharing on Facebook

I think one of the best ways to have fun when you're learning something like this is to play show and tell, so I'd recommend going on Facebook and sharing your new blog.

For the teachers out there: classes that are learning WordPress might like to make a Facebook page and have everyone post their blog posts to the Facebook page as a gathering point. To learn about Facebook pages, see www.facebook.com/help/?page=175 or http://tinyurl.com/fbhelp-pages.

What you'll need to do is to select and copy the link in your browser window. It might be something like this.

Or you could just select the first portion: http://wordpressprimer.wordpress.com.

Then get on Facebook, and look for the What's on Your Mind box.

Type in a message, paste your link, and click the Share button (see Figure 3.11).

Figure 3.11
Posting a blog to Facebook.

Then you should see something like this. Your blog will go to all of your Facebook friends, courtesy of the News Feed.

Yeehaw! That was fun.

CONCLUSION

Dear Reader,

A very special congratulations on making your WordPress blog!

You're now ready to inspire, entertain, or admonish the world with your writing!

In the next chapter, we'll look at a few more things you might want to try, including working with digital images.

As always, feel free to visit www.wordpressprimer.net/blogs and view other readers' blogs, or share a link to your blog.

Also, if you're on Facebook, you can visit the companion Facebook page, where you can participate in discussions with other people who are learning WordPress. See http://tinyurl.com/wpp-fb.

Regards,

Todd

CHAPTER 4

WORKING WITH DIGITAL IMAGES

In This Chapter:

- Fine-Tuning Images While Uploading in WordPress
- Using a Picture from Facebook in a Blog Post
- Resizing Pictures from Picresize.com
- Online Image Editing with Picnik.com
- Managing Photos with Picasa
- Renaming Pictures on Your Computer

The purpose of this chapter is to consider a few techniques that might be helpful for working with images for your blog. Some people blog entirely in words, but visuals can certainly help develop and maintain interest. They can also be something you write about.

WordPress has some built-in capability to adjust images as they are being uploaded. You can also use tools to adjust images online or on your computer. It can be helpful to learn a bit about how digital images are sized, especially if you have a digital camera that shoots high-quality pictures. When you are using pictures online, you don't necessarily need all the megapixels a camera can provide. Extra megapixels can result in longer upload times, and there may not be a benefit; resizing a picture can make things easier.

Also, we'll take a quick peek at Picasa, which can be a powerful tool for working with images. It's easy to use, free, and has a lot of great features. I highly recommend it.

FINE-TUNING IMAGES WHILE UPLOADING IN WORDPRESS

You can make certain adjustments to images as part of the uploading process, but there are other adjustments you can make once an image is uploaded.

To try out these features, log in and click New Post. (Please review the previous chapter on posting if necessary.)

Then click the Select Files button, locate an image you want to upload, and double-click on it to begin the upload process.

If you'd like a large picture to use as an example, see www.wordpressprimer.net/files.

Depending on the speed of your Internet connection and the size of the file, you'll get a progress bar.

Then, in the Add an Image window, use the scrollbar on the right side to scroll down so that you can see the title and other fields shown (see Figure 4.1).

None of these fields is required, but if you like, you can enter information to help you keep track of the pictures in WordPress and to add extra detail (see Figure 4.2). The fields, shown in the figure, follow:

■ **Title.** A title for the image for keeping track of it in WordPress.

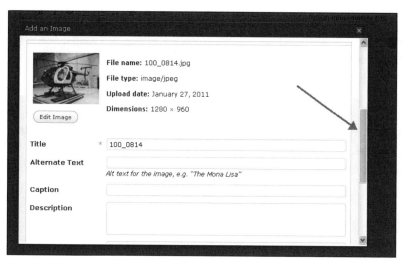

Figure 4.1
Scrolling in the Add an Image window.

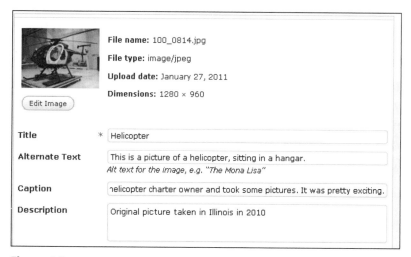

Figure 4.2
Adjusting image info.

- **Alternate Text.** Entering a basic description allows visually impaired people to have a sense of what is in the picture; the alt text provides screen readers with a text alternative.

- **Caption.** Enter something here if you want a caption to appear beneath the picture in a blog post.

▪ **Description.** WordPress has a thing called an *attachment page*, which is a view of a picture that allows you to display an extended description if you like. In the next section, you learn how to have people go to this page when they click on the picture so they can see a full-size version of the image.

Scroll down farther in the Add an Image window. This next set of options allows you to control whether the image appears on the left, in the center, or on the right; it also allows you to change the size of the image and adjust the link URL.

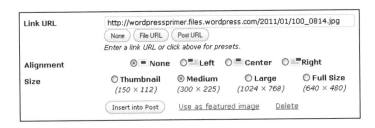

If you click None under Link URL, the picture appears at the size you set, but nothing happens when you click on it. The default setting is File URL, which simply means when you click on the picture, you see the original size version of it. If you click Post URL, when people click on the picture, they go to the attachments page for the post.

You might want to set a series of pictures to a smaller size (such as a thumbnail) if there are a lot of them but then allow people to click and see bigger versions of them. In that case, captions might not be necessary, but you might want a description to appear when people click on the image. You might enter something in the Description field, click Thumbnail for size, and then click the Post URL button.

The best way to learn is to try. Click on everything, insert images, and publish posts. Have fun with it!

The Size option defaults to Medium. The Large option in this case is the original size of the picture, which would be a bit big for the screen. I think 640 × 480 is a nice size for pictures.

After you make your adjustments, click the Insert into Post button.

Then, on the right side of the Dashboard screen, click the Publish button.

Click View Post. Woohoo! The image appears, and if you've added a caption, it appears beneath it.

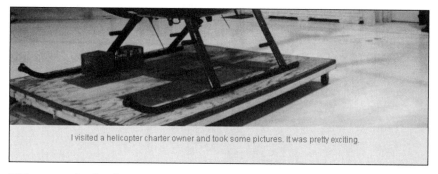

When you're looking at a post on your blog, as long as you're signed in, you can go back and change something by scrolling down to the bottom of the post and clicking the Edit link.

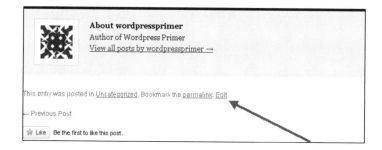

Now we'll look at editing images that have been inserted in a post. There are some additional things we can do.

To start, simply click on the image in the post (see Figure 4.3).

Figure 4.3
You can click on the image in the post.

Two little icons appear in the upper-left corner. The one on the right allows you to delete an image with a single click.

Click the icon on the left, which provides some picture adjustment capability and leads to the Edit Image tab.

This technique is probably the easiest way to resize and adjust an image, including any captions, once it is already posted. The Edit Image tab has a number of options in it, as you can see from Figure 4.4. One option that doesn't

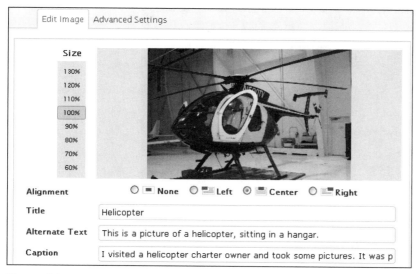

Figure 4.4
You can adjust the size of the image by clicking on percentage values on the left.

appear when uploading is the vertical Size bar, which allows you to easily change the size of the image.

To change the size of the image, roll your mouse pointer over different percentages. When you find one you like, click on it.

Then scroll down to the bottom of the Add an Image window, and click the Update button (see Figure 4.5).

To explore further adjustments you can make, click the Advanced Settings tab.

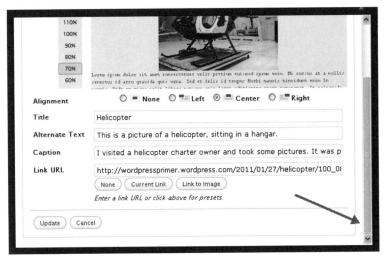

Figure 4.5
Scrolling down to get to the Update button.

You can tweak various image settings here. Try entering a number like 1 in the Border field. This adds a border around an image, which can be a nice effect, especially if you have a picture or image with a lot of white or lighter colors around the edge.

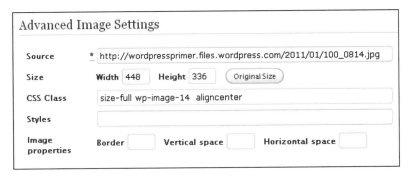

Next, scroll down a bit more; these settings are useful generally only if you are getting deeper into learning Hypertext Markup Language (HTML) code or Cascading Style Sheets (CSS). Both of these are "languages" you can use to tweak your blog. (If you're interested in learning more about these, you might like to explore www.w3schools.com/html or www.w3schools.com/css and then try clicking on the HTML tab when you're composing a post.)

When you're ready to move on, click the Update button.

Advanced Link Settings	
Title	
Link Rel	attachment wp-att-14
CSS Class	
Styles	
Target	Open link in a new window ☐

(Update) (Cancel)

Using a Picture from Facebook in a Blog Post

There's no right or wrong way to work with images. If you have digital pictures on your computer that are organized well, you can just upload them directly to a blog post. But maybe you're not sure where a specific picture is. You know you have it in a Facebook photo album, and you'd like to use it in a blog post.

The first step in using a picture from Facebook is to find it in a photo album (see Figure 4.6).

Figure 4.6
A photo in a Facebook photo album.

Once you find the picture you want, one option is to right-click (Windows) or Ctrl-click (Mac) and download the image to your computer in a location where you can locate it for uploading.

Another option is to right-click (Windows) or Ctrl-click (Mac) and select Copy Image Location. This option places the link to the image in memory, allowing you to then place that in a blog post and point to the image. It doesn't mean someone is going to get to the photo album; it's just a way to display the picture in WordPress without having to upload an image into the post.

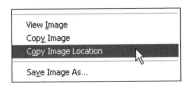

Note

The appearance of the menu is shown as it would look in Windows, using Firefox. If you use Internet Explorer or Chrome, this option might be worded differently.

So if you try this technique and paste the text somewhere, the link looks something like this:

http://sphotos.ak.fbcdn.net/hphotos-ak-ash1/
hs319.ash1/28106_392669344569_773814569_3879678_2531954_n.png

The idea is that you do this in one tab on your browser or one window, and you have your blog post open in the other window/tab. Then you can paste the link into the blog post as part of adding an image.

So go to a post on your blog and follow the procedure for adding an image as shown previously, up until this point. Then click on the From URL tab.

What you're doing, instead of uploading the image, is pasting a link.

Click in the Image URL field, and paste the link. If it doesn't paste, go back to the other window/tab where the image is, right-click/Ctrl-click and copy the image location again, come back, and try pasting again.

Then scroll down and click Insert into Post.

Insert into Post

If all goes well, your post will look just like you've uploaded an image.

RESIZING PICTURES WITH PICRESIZE.COM

If you like, you can upload pictures into WordPress at whatever size they are, even if they're big files. If you have a high-speed Internet connection and the upload speed of your Internet connection is good, this technique might be fine.

But there are some reasons you might want to consider sizing images before you upload them. One would be if your Internet connection is not particularly fast. Other reasons include the fact that you have a limited amount of image space in a WordPress blog; it's a fair amount, such as 3 gigabytes (3,000 megabytes), but over time, you can eat that up.

Also, if you like the idea of having larger versions of pictures for people to see when they click on the picture in the blog post, you probably won't want to have a 5,000-pixel-wide image.

For example, if your camera is super-duper-megapixel capable, you might have a 5,000-pixel-wide image that you upload. WordPress automatically makes the preview image in the post smaller. But if someone clicks on the picture, they see a picture that's so big that only a small portion of it can be seen at any one time.

So you might want to experiment with resizing pictures before you upload them to 600 or 800 pixels wide. A variety of programs can do this. One of the easiest options is www.picresize.com. To try it, visit www.picresize.com, click on the Browse button to locate a picture on your computer, and double-click on it. (Feel free to try downloading one of the pictures on www.wordpressprimer.net/files.)

After you've selected the picture, click the Continue button.

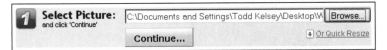

There will be various things you can try (see Figure 4.7). I suggest clicking on everything!

Figure 4.7
Some of the options in picresize.com.

After you have some fun, you can scroll down and try clicking on the Resize Your Picture drop-down menu (see Figure 4.8). Or maybe you'll get distracted by trying one of the special effects and clicking on the Load Live Preview button!

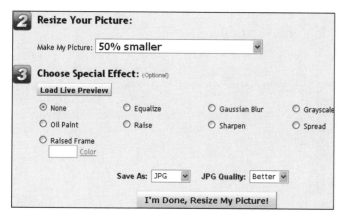

Figure 4.8
Resizing options and special effects.

You can choose a percentage, but I like to choose Custom Size.

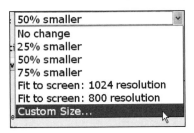

Then I like to choose Pixels from the drop-down menu. A *pixel* is a building block for an image.

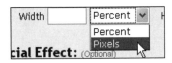

Then you can enter something like 600 or 800 in the Width field.

You don't need to enter anything for Height.

Then click I'm Done, Resize My Picture.

I'm Done, Resize My Picture!

Picresize.com chews on the image, and then it gives you some more options. Notice how it indicates the relative file size of an image.

As always, I recommend clicking on everything.

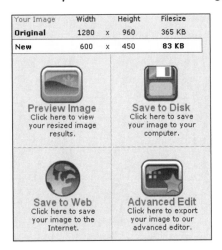

In particular, you might enjoy clicking on Advanced Edit.

The Advanced Edit mode leads to a number of functions that would be similar to programs you might have on a computer, like Photoshop (see Figure 4.9). You get extra credit for trying them all! Oh wait—I'm not teaching a class. Well, you can have extra credit anyway, courtesy of Dr. Fun! (That's me.)

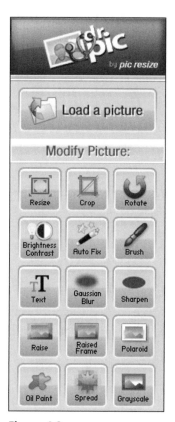

Figure 4.9
Options in the Modify Picture panel.

ONLINE IMAGE EDITING WITH PICNIK.COM

Another online image editing tool you might enjoy trying or at least filing away is www.picnik.com.

It's kind of like www.picresize.com, but it has some more advanced features and some fun options (see Figure 4.10). There's also a nice feature that allows you to

Figure 4.10
Picnik.com can integrate with popular places to put pictures.

tap into places where you might already have pictures, grab them, and edit them. (See the bottom part of the screenshot.)

To try Picnik, click Get Started Now.

Picnik then starts loading the application and has some pithy descriptions underneath the progress bar to keep you distracted while you wait for it to load.

When it's ready, click the Upload a Photo button.

This is another situation where I recommend clicking on everything to explore and have fun (see Figure 4.11).

You might also like to try the Create tab (see Figure 4.12). It has some things for teachers or parents who want to add some fun to family pictures or pictures for events. For example, if you click one of the options on the left, such as Confetti

Figure 4.11
Some of the Edit options in picnik.com.

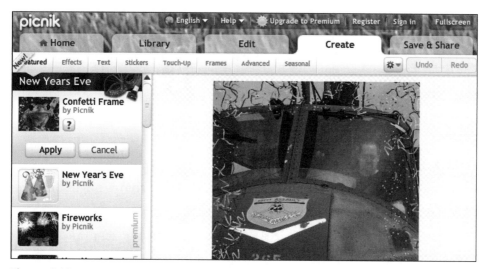

Figure 4.12
Some of the special effects you can apply to a picture.

Frame, it adds a playful border to a picture. Then you can click the Apply button if you like it, or click Cancel if you don't.

When you're done playing, you can click the Save & Share tab.

If you forgot to apply a special affect, Picnik prompts you before it continues. If you'd like to add the effect permanently to the picture (not the original copy that you uploaded, but to the one you're creating), click Apply. Or click Discard if you want to save the picture without the effect, or Cancel.

Then click Save Photo.

Picnik also lets you do things like adding a picture to a mug or a card. Woohoo!

Managing Photos with Picasa

I highly recommend that you explore Picasa, a free tool from Google that you can download and run. See www.google.com/picasa.

Picasa is a powerful picture manager that can automatically scan and import pictures whenever you load them on your computer. It allows you to make slideshows and helps you connect to online places to share your pictures. (There's also a nice plugin for Facebook that allows you to work with pictures in Picasa and then upload with a click to Facebook. Try Googling `facebook plugin picasa`.)

One of the things I have been most impressed with in Picasa is the Fill Light feature, which has an impressive ability to adjust the brightness of pictures (see

Figure 4.13). It goes beyond adjusting brightness/contrast and allows you to tweak very nicely.

Figure 4.13
The Fill Light feature in Picasa is pretty impressive.

You just pull up a picture and click on the little slider bar.

And it does wonders. It's hard to do it justice in a printed or electronic book—the best way to see it in action is to try it out directly.

RENAMING PICTURES ON YOUR COMPUTER

Before we wrap up this chapter, I want to mention one more thing. With so many pictures floating around, it's understandable that digital cameras only assign numbers to images, but the numbers can make it a challenge to keep track of them, much less to know which file to upload to Facebook or a blog post.

So you might have a picture file that looks like this:

At the very least, you might want to learn with your operating system how to enable thumbnails.

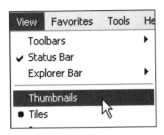

That way, when you are browsing through files on your computer, you can have some idea of what the pictures are.

100_0814.jpg

The challenge is that when you're uploading to something like WordPress, when you come back to upload, you might not see thumbnail images. You might see just filenames.

One thing you can do with pictures is rename the files from numbers to something more useful. Just right-click (Windows) or Ctrl-click (Mac) and choose the Rename option.

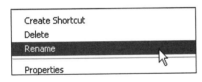

The filename will probably be selected.

Then you can just type a new name.

N o t e

It's really important that if you are renaming a file, and it has a .jpg, .png, or .gif at the end, you preserve that ending; otherwise, your computer may get confused and no longer recognize it as an image.

After renaming, instead of seeing a list like this

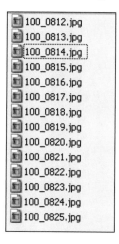

you have named files that are easy to locate.

heather at work.jpg
heather at the beach.jpg
heather at a meeting.jpg
heather in outer space.jpg
how to destroy your computer.jpg
karen at a kenny rogers concert.jpg
ronald reagan and a chimpanzee.jpg

CONCLUSION

Dear Reader,

Whoo-whee! Congratulations on making it to the end of this chapter. There are a lot of fun things you can go back and try from this chapter. And if you're thinking that you want to promote and grow your blog as much as possible, I recommend that you think about visuals whenever possible.

You might make friends with a photographer (try joining Flickr.com and looking for photographers there), or you might just try taking pictures yourself.

Another option to consider is a site like www.publicdomainpictures.net.

As you're working on posts and learning things, feel free to share a link to a post on the WordPress Primer Facebook Page: http://tinyurl.com/wpp-fb.

Best wishes in your digital image adventures!

Regards,

Todd

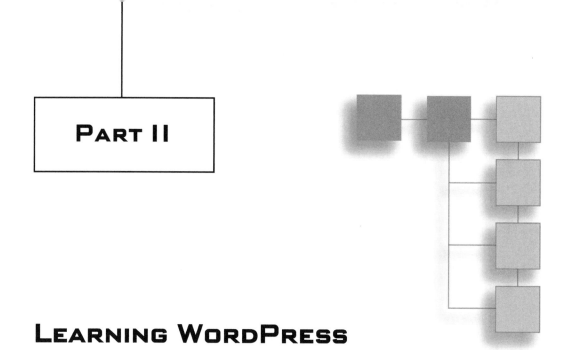

PART II

LEARNING WORDPRESS

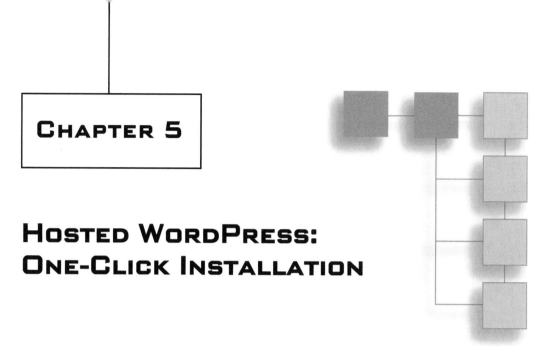

CHAPTER 5

HOSTED WORDPRESS: ONE-CLICK INSTALLATION

In This Chapter:

- Starting a Hosting Account
- Installing WordPress with QuickInstall
- Extra: Redeeming AdWords Credit

The purpose of this chapter is to show you how easy it can be to get a WordPress site going using a quick installer.

In the past, you pretty much needed to hire a developer or learn some serious technical skills to install a content management system.

To have a fully customizable, hosted WordPress site, you need to have an Internet hosting account. The example company we're using is HostGator, which is a popular hosting company offering good prices and a great quick installer. The company also occasionally runs deals where you can get $100 in AdWords credit. AdWords is Google's advertising platform, and it's a nice way to get some attention for your blog or website. Later in this book when we look at promoting your site, we'll look at Facebook advertising and Google AdWords.

STARTING A HOSTING ACCOUNT

To start a hosting account, visit www.hostgator.com. It will look something like this.

Click View Web Hosting Plans. To start, I recommend going with a "Hatchling" plan. If you know you're going to want this website for at least a year, you can save by paying ahead of time. Prices may vary, but at the time of writing, it's $4.95/month. By going with the monthly option, you can try things out but cancel if you don't like it.

Then when you're ready, click Order Now.

There's a lot of information on the next page, but the most interesting to me is when the site runs deals on getting free Google AdWords credit. You can scroll down and check to see if HostGator is running a deal.

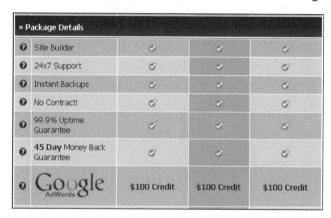

When you're finished, scroll up and click the Close link.

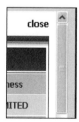

Step 1 involves website names. If you're just learning, I'd recommend picking a name for practice; don't worry about it too much, because the cost for website names is only around $10 per year. You can come up with an idea for a name on the left, and you can click the little drop-down .com and choose other endings, if the name you want is not available. If you do want to get your own, new name, you can also go to register.com and see what's available (but don't register there). Then you can start the account at HostGator when you've found one you like that is available.

Or, if you already have a name registered somewhere else, you can always point it to a new account. It's like cell phone portability. If you get a new phone, you still own the number and can point it at a new phone. Also, be aware that when you register a domain name, it's separate from hosting. That is, if you start an account somewhere and register a name, and you also have hosting, you can keep the name but ditch the hosting. A website name is a domain name. You can have a domain-only account.

At any rate, if you have a website name already, just enter it on the right, and then keep in mind that there will be things you need to do at your registrar account or domain account (the place where you registered the website name) to repoint it. Contact your registrar/hosting company where you registered the name, and ask how to point it to HostGator. When you get a confirmation email from HostGator, it will have a couple lines that are called *nameservers*. Basically, you end up needing to point your website name toward those servers.

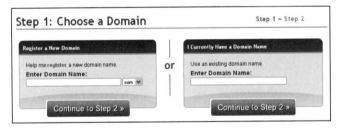

When you're ready, click Continue to Step 2, and finish the process of starting your account. At some point you'll get a confirmation email. The Control Panel link is the one you'll use to log into your account. The email will also have your username and password. Print it or write it down!

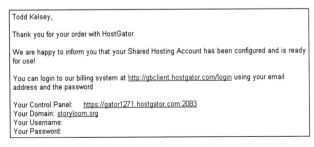

Installing WordPress with QuickInstall

This quick installation stuff is really quite fantastic.

You can use your Control Panel to log directly into your account, or you might be able to visit your website name and then click the cPanel Login on a screen that looks something like the one shown here (see Figure 5.1).

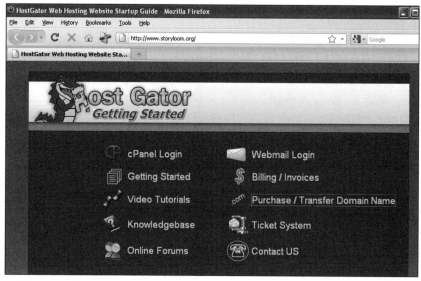

Figure 5.1
The first time you look at your site, a set of Getting Started links may appear.

Use the username/password provided in the email. You might also want to bookmark the Control Panel (cPanel) login.

The first time you log in, if you want to learn more about your hosting account, you can click the Get Started Now button when this little window pops up, or you can click the View Our Video Tutorials link.

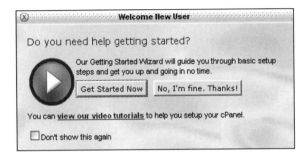

The cPanel screen has lots of goodies on it. Scroll all the way down to the Software/Services section, and click QuickInstall.

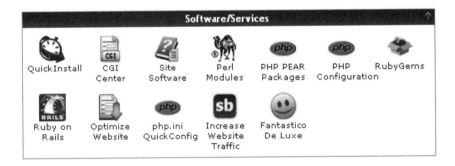

The QuickInstall logo appears at the top of the screen. It's worth noting that this is one area where you can come back and manage your quick installations. You might want to bookmark it.

Then scroll down to the Blog Software section, and click on WordPress.

When this next screen comes up, click the Continue button.

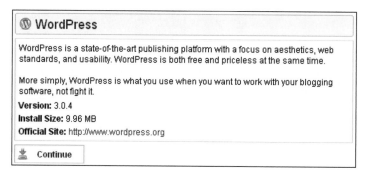

This next screen provides some different options. If your website name hasn't been connected yet, there might be a temporary address you can use. The section that starts with http:// allows you to place WordPress at a specific address. If you leave the field on the right blank, WordPress is installed at your website address. In my case, that's fine. When people type in `storyloom.org`, they're directed to WordPress.

But if you want, you can enter something like `blog` on the right.

Because I'm doing that, QuickInstall places WordPress at http://storyloom.org/blog. Generally speaking, if you're experimenting and want to try other content management systems that are available under QuickInstall, you can place some test installations at addresses like Drupal or Joomla or CMS and then access them at those addresses (for example, websitename.com/drupal or websitename.com/joomla). There may be limitations in how many you can do, but if you can delete a QuickInstall, it might be a fun way to try out different systems.

Note

If you have a general company or organization website like www.mycompany.com, you can ask your hosting company how to make a subdomain, such as http://blog.mycompany.com. If you own the website name, you can always do *something*.websitename.com, such as http://blog.websitename.com. If your main purpose is to use a website name for the blog, www.myblogname.com is fine. But it's helpful to note that you can always create a subdomain and point it at a QuickInstall. Ask support at your hosting company.

In the install window, enter an email address for the admin email—that is, the main one to be used with the WordPress account. Then choose a title for the blog, and click the Install Now button.

A progress bar displays.

44%

You should get a congratulations message. You'll probably want to click the Here link and bookmark it, and then check your email address.

Congratulations!

Your installation is ready. You can access it now by going here. If there is any login information, it will have been sent to the email address you provided.

You should get an email that looks something like this.

☐ ☆ no-reply   **Successful installation** · Your new WordPress site has been successfully set up at: http://storyloom.org/blog   2:25 pm

The email itself will look something like this.

The email will have a username and password, which is your WordPress username/password. It's what you use to log into WordPress as an administrator.

Woohoo! WordPress is installed!

Visit the link provided in the confirmation email. Your blog should look something like Figure 5.2.

Figure 5.2
A newly created blog.

Next, scroll down and click the Log In link, and enter the username/password to log in to WordPress.

When you're logged in, you may want to bookmark the Dashboard in your browser; depending on your website name and where you installed WordPress, the admin link looks something like this.

The Dashboard appears. It should be similar to the free version of WordPress (see Figure 5.3).

Figure 5.3
The WordPress Dashboard.

One of the differences that we'll explore in subsequent chapters is the ability to use plugins. But some of the customization you can do applies to both free and hosted versions of WordPress.

In the next chapter, we look at a super-critical thing: security. It's important to know how to upgrade WordPress, because if you don't, a hacker could compromise your website, and you could lose everything.

We also look at a fact of life of working with blogs: comment spam.

The rest of this chapter is devoted to some extras, like taking advantage of AdWords. If you're lucky, HostGator will be offering a promotion for free AdWords. If you want to use AdWords, don't put the promotion off, because it might have an expiration date.

You'll probably want to start an AdWords account to promote your website. There are various ways to learn how to use AdWords, such as by reading the Help section in Google AdWords or reading the free ebook *AdWords Primer* (www.adwordsprimer.com).

EXTRA: REDEEMING ADWORDS CREDIT

So if you started a hosting account at HostGator and *if* there's a promotion running, when you log into the Control Panel, you see a box like this.

And when you click the Redeem Now link, you come across a page like this (see Figure 5.4).

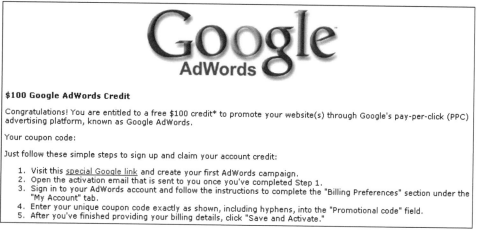

Figure 5.4
The AdWords Credit page.

Bookmark this screen, and write down your coupon code. It has been blanked out of the picture above, but this is the screen where it appears, and you need it for later. I recommend copying and pasting it into an email to yourself. Also, you might need to wait as long as 24 hours before you can use the code.

The instructions on this page are important. Read the entire page, including the fine print, that will be something like this:

Promotional credit must be applied to a new AdWords account within 15 days of creating the account.

This means you need to be on the ball and complete all these steps within 15 days of creating the new AdWords account.

Here's some additional information that appears on one of the screens.

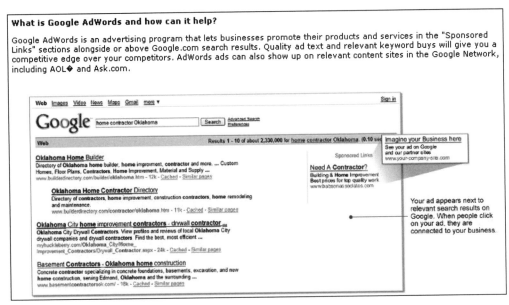

When you're ready, click the Start My Free AdWords Trial Now button.

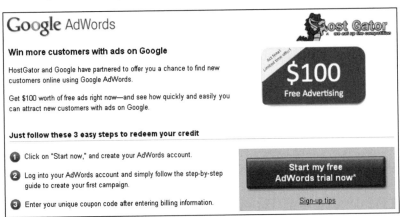

I recommend creating/using a Gmail address for AdWords because it's easier to get around that way. You can set the Gmail address to forward incoming email to another address if you want. Just go to Mail Settings (Gear icon in upper-right corner of screen) > Forwarding and POP/IMAP > Forward a Copy of Incoming Mail to (*choose email*) > Save Changes.

There's also a short video you might like to look at.

Then when you're ready to start your account, this next screen allows you to enter contact information so you can get some free help on how to use AdWords.

But if you don't want to be contacted, just click Continue without filling information out.

Then click I Have an Email Address and Password I Already Use with Google Services Like AdSense, Gmail, Orkut, or iGoogle (if you've created a Gmail address).

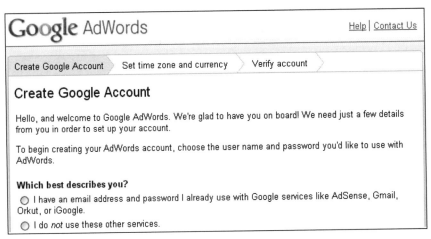

Then another question appears, and you can choose either option. If you click the first option, you see a window that allows you to enter your Gmail address and password so that AdWords can link to your existing Gmail account (see Figure 5.5).

Figure 5.5
Choosing which Google account to use.

By the way, there's no monthly fee or anything with AdWords. You just pay for ads you run. But if you try it out, be aware of the start and end date of your ad campaign and your daily budget (to make sure AdWords doesn't drain your bank account).

Next, choose your time zone and currency preferences, and click the Continue button.

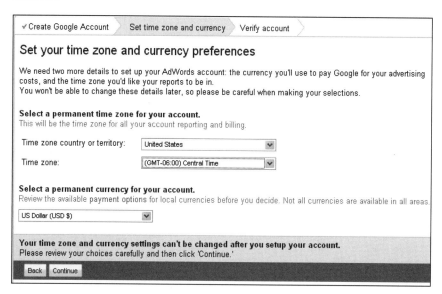

After your account has been created, you can click Sign In to Your AdWords Account, or you can go to google.com/adwords in the future.

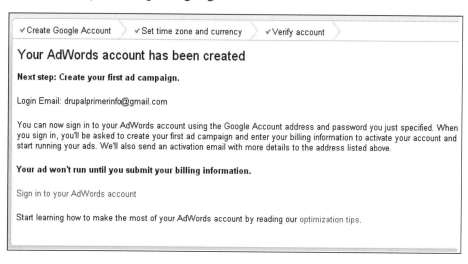

To redeem the credit from a promotion, sign into AdWords and click the Billing menu and the Billing Preferences option.

Here are the original instructions from the promotional page we visited earlier.

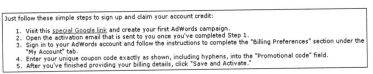

When you visit the Billing Preferences option, if it is the first time you've visited, you see an Account Setup screen, where you need to select your country and click Continue.

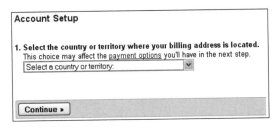

Then you need to enter your basic contact information and click Continue.

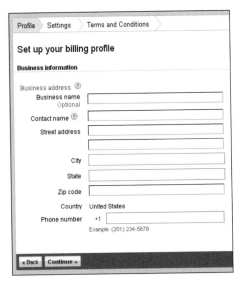

Next, you arrive at a payment options screen. Entering credit card info is not optional, and there is a $5.00 activation fee, but it may be applied to your account anyway. (See the little question mark at the bottom of the screen.)

A question appears at the bottom of the screen: Do you have a promotion code? This is where you enter the coupon code from the earlier screen (see Figure 5.6).

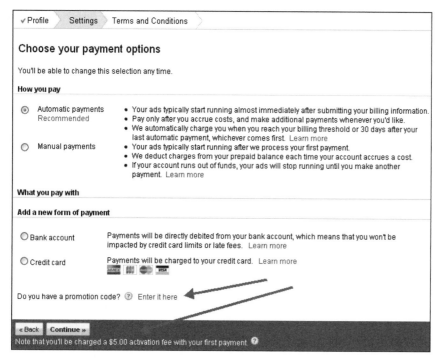

Figure 5.6
The page where you can enter a promotion code.

Then when you're ready, click Continue, and you're ready to explore AdWords, which Chapter 14, "Promoting with Social Advertising," looks at. You can also learn more about AdWords by visiting the Help section when you sign into AdWords. Or you might be interested in checking out the AdWords Primer at www.adwordsprimer.com.

CONCLUSION

Dear Reader,

Congratulations on installing WordPress!

In subsequent chapters, whenever plugins are discussed, they apply generally to the hosted version of WordPress (although the free version comes with some built-in plugins; you just can't add any). Then we look at customization options that apply to both free and hosted sites.

If you want to share the link to your new blog, please feel free to come and visit the WordPress Primer Facebook Page at www.facebook.com/pages/wordpressprimer/186134644744074 or http://tinyurl.com/wpp-fb.

To see some examples of blogs people have done on WordPress, visit www.wordpressprimer.net/links.

Regards,

Todd

Chapter 6

Spam, Spam, Spam, Spam: Understanding Spam and Security for WordPress

In This Chapter:

- The Bridge of Death: Ignore This Chapter and Be Sent to the Gorge of Eternal Peril
- Adjusting Comment/Spam Settings
- Trying Out Akismet: Spam Killer
- Updating WordPress So You Don't Lose Everything
- Backing Up WordPress
- Installing a Plugin: BackupWordPress
- Exploring BlogBooker

The purpose of this chapter is to help you learn more about security and spam. Because this is not the most fun topic in the world, I'll try to spice things up a bit. Before computers were around, there was the canned spam, so we'll start there: the namesake of comment/blog spam.

To start, I recommend watching this video by the comedy troupe Monty Python, which is a sing-along version to the canned version of spam: http://tinyurl.com/montyspam.

Next, you might like to visit www.spam.com. (Vegetarian readers may substitute this site visit by searching for and visiting the Morningstar Farms website.)

And, if you dare, visit the Spam Brand History link.

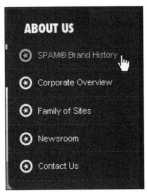

Or you might like to plan a personal or class visit to the Spam Museum in Austin, Minnesota.

And now, for something completely different, we get to the most important part of the chapter.

THE BRIDGE OF DEATH: IGNORE THIS CHAPTER AND BE SENT TO THE GORGE OF ETERNAL PERIL

I have attempted to lure you into actually reading this chapter using various tactics, knowing that security is the last thing that you probably want to think about. Here are a few reasons you might like to read and act on this entire chapter:

- Comment spam can be really, really annoying. Read the subsequent sections if you're not sure what comment spam is.

- Comment spam can take up a lot of your time. And that's time better spent on blogging or _____.

- Security is important if you don't want to lose everything. There are some relatively easy ways to protect your blog, and the more thoughts you put into it, the more precious it will become. So I highly recommend becoming acquainted with a few techniques.

- BlogBooker, mentioned at the end of the chapter (no peeking!) is a really nice way to make another kind of backup of your blog. Not only does it result in a printable ebook, it's a way to preserve your blog for future generations.

Okay. You've reached another milestone: reading this far into the chapter. Congratulations!

To discover what the heading of this section of the chapter is referring to, please visit the following YouTube video: http://tinyurl.com/bridgeofdeath. It describes where you will be sent if you do not read and act upon this entire chapter.

Understanding Blog Comment Spam

Okay, so one of the nice things about blogging is the comments feature. It's partly why people read blogs: so they can have the opportunity to "sound off" on them.

For example, on your new blog, if you have comments enabled (you can turn this feature off if you like; see the "Adjusting Comment/Spam Settings" section),

someone can click and fill out a form and leave a comment.

The problem is that spammers out there have automated programs that scan for and try to identify WordPress sites and then leave comments with links for advertisements. This can be pretty annoying, because it's like your field of flowers all the sudden has a bunch of weeds sprouting up every day. You end up getting email notifications and having to go in and decide whether to delete comments.

Suffice it to say, it's worth learning about ways to reduce, and ideally eliminate, as much of this comment spam as possible, so that you can have the (real) benefit of comment-based discussion without as much hassle.

At this point, ask yourself, "What if I made a Facebook page and used the Notes feature to post notes instead of a blog?" There's far less customization available on a Facebook page, but it's an alternative to file away. If you want another distraction, try it. Go to www.facebook.com/pages and click Create Page at the top right. Then when your page is set up, try writing a Note. Guess what you get? The ability for people to *comment*. Hmmm. There are many things you can't do on a Facebook Note that you can with a WordPress blog (A WordPress blog is much more customizable), but a Facebook page might be something to file away and compare and contrast with a blog.

Understanding Blog Security

When you have your own hosted WordPress blog, it's not automatically updated. Some hacker may discover a new way to get into a WordPress blog, and WordPress might release a security update to cover it—kind of like the way Windows or Mac operating systems are sometimes updated for security.

This is one difference between the customized, hosted WordPress and the free WordPress. The free WordPress is updated for you. With the customized WordPress, you get the customization—the ability to add whatever plugins you like, which can increase the sophistication of the blog. The downside is that you need to update WordPress yourself when a security upgrade comes up. So it's a trade-off.

If you don't update WordPress, you risk a hacker coming in and deleting everything on your blog.

ADJUSTING COMMENT/SPAM SETTINGS

So now we'll start taking some action, so you can avoid the Gorge of Eternal Peril!

To explore settings you can adjust, log into your blog. (You can visit it and click the Log In link toward the bottom.)

Then click on Dashboard.

And click on Settings.

The Settings area has a variety of things to play around with. I recommend exploring all of them! When you're ready to cross the Bridge of Death, click the Discussion link.

The Discussion area has a lot of settings that might not initially mean anything to you, but eventually, you'll probably want to come back and tweak things.

For example, some people may want to uncheck the setting that allows people to post comments on new articles. If you disable this feature, you don't get any spam, but you also get no comments. This is the setting that Jack Bauer of

24 would use to close down a WordPress blog when comment spam was presenting a threat to national security.

Discussion Settings

Default article settings	☑ Attempt to notify any blogs linked to from the article.
	☑ Allow link notifications from other blogs (pingbacks and trackbacks.)
	☑ Allow people to post comments on new articles
	(These settings may be overridden for individual articles.)

After you've been blogging for a while, you might like to try tweaking Other Comment Settings.

Other comment settings	☑ Comment author must fill out name and e-mail
	☐ Users must be registered and logged in to comment
	☐ Automatically close comments on articles older than 14 days
	☑ Enable threaded (nested) comments 5 ▼ levels deep
	☐ Break comments into pages with 50 top level comments per page and the
	last ▼ page displayed by default
	Comments should be displayed with the older ▼ comments at the top of each page

This is a section you'll want to be very familiar with. If you like, you can receive an email whenever someone posts a comment. Some comments may be held for moderation. If so, you can receive an email when one is held for approval (a situation where you need to go in and approve it before it can be seen). On a related note, in the Before a Comment Appears section, you can set the options for your needing to approve any comment before it appears.

E-mail me whenever	☑ Anyone posts a comment
	☑ A comment is held for moderation
Before a comment appears	☐ An administrator must always approve the comment
	☑ Comment author must have a previously approved comment

You can tweak the Comment Moderation setting related to the number of links that are included in a comment. There is a text field where you can enter specific words, links, or email addresses if you want to moderate a comment coming from a particular person or that contains a particular word. An *IP address* is the computer location, something like 232.121.552.121. It's kind of like a phone number, but for computer networks. When comments are made, or if you know of someone's IP address, you can use it to screen comments.

| Comment Moderation | Hold a comment in the queue if it contains 2   or more links. (A common characteristic of comment spam is a large number of hyperlinks.) |
| | When a comment contains any of these words in its content, name, URL, e-mail, or IP, it will be held in the moderation queue. One word or IP per line. It will match inside words, so "press" will match "WordPress". |

The Comment Blacklist function works similarly to the Comment Moderation function; in this case, you can entirely block words, addresses, emails, and more by entering them here.

Comment Blacklist	When a comment contains any of these words in its content, name, URL, e-mail, or IP, it will be marked as spam. One word or IP per line. It will match inside words, so "press" will match "WordPress".

When you're done adjusting Discussion Settings, click Save Changes.

TRYING OUT AKISMET: SPAM KILLER

Akismet is a plugin for WordPress that can help automatically reduce/block comment spam. Akismet might be bundled with WordPress when you start your account. (If it isn't, search for `akismet WordPress plugin` on Google, download it, and follow the instructions for installing and activating a plugin found later in this chapter.)

To try out Akismet, click on your Dashboard.

Select the Plugins button.

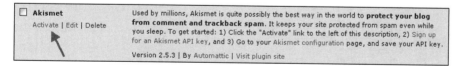

And in the list of plugins, click the Activate link next to Akismet.

☐ **Akismet**
Activate | Edit | Delete

Used by millions, Akismet is quite possibly the best way in the world to **protect your blog from comment and trackback spam**. It keeps your site protected from spam even while you sleep. To get started: 1) Click the "Activate" link to the left of this description, 2) Sign up for an Akismet API key, and 3) Go to your Akismet configuration page, and save your API key.

Version 2.5.3 | By Automattic | Visit plugin site

Then come back and click the Settings link.

You need to go through a few hoops to get Akismet running. It's free for personal use (although you're asked for a donation), and there's a charge for any type of commercial use (that is, if you're making money by using it). Akismet is a popular plugin for WordPress, so it's probably worth jumping through the hoops. If you don't jump now, don't be surprised if you come back and jump through the hoops after you start getting a bunch of comment spam.

In the settings area, click on the Get Your Key link. It's a code that activates Akismet and allows your blog to talk to the Akismet servers to discuss spam.

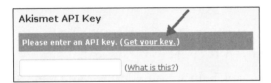

And you might want to right-click (Windows) or Ctrl-click (Mac) and select Open Link in New Tab, which leaves your Dashboard intact on the Akismet Settings screen.

On the Akismet site, click Get an Akismet API Key.

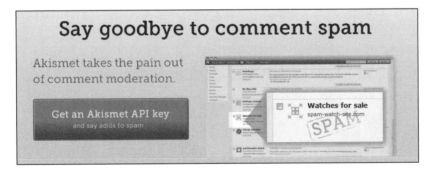

Then click the Sign Up link in the Personal Site section (see Figure 6.1).

Click on the slider, where it shows a price and a happy face expectantly hoping for a donation, and drag it to the left (unless you do want to make a donation) (see Figure 6.2).

Figure 6.1
Choosing the Sign Up link in the Personal Site section at Akismet.

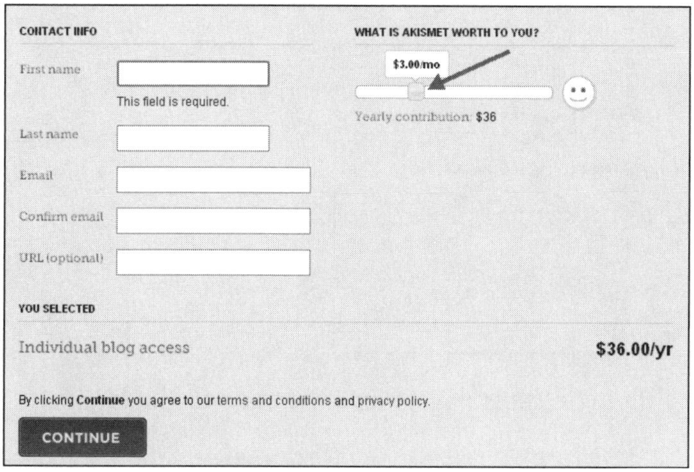

Figure 6.2
Clicking and dragging the price slider.

If you can bear the sad face at $0.00/mo, fill out your contact info and click the Continue button (see Figure 6.3).

You will receive an email with the code, called an API key, which you can select and copy.

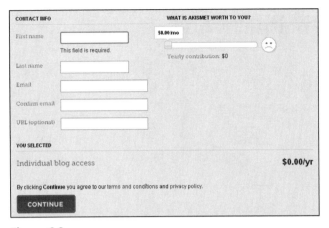

Figure 6.3
Filling out contact information.

The API key will be something like sskcj334asdd. Just select the letters/numbers, not the space before or after the code, and copy it into memory (Ctrl+C).

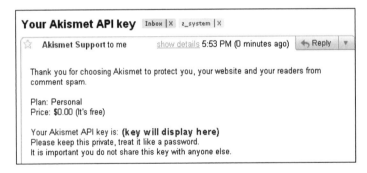

Then back on the Akismet Plugin Settings page, paste the code in the blank text field.

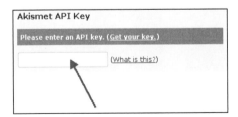

And click on the Update Options button.

You should receive a confirmation message.

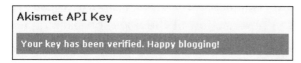

There are various settings you can tweak and more things you can learn, which might become increasingly important when you get more traffic or have spam issues. Try visiting the Akismet site for more information: http://akismet.com/.

If you run into any issues (such as your blog not loading for some reason), try deactivating Akismet. I had this issue, and deactivating it, visiting the blog page, and then reactivating it seemed to help. Akismet might cause loading issues for a blog, especially with the free version, or your hosting company could be having a bad day. If you want to use Akismet and continue to have issues, contact support for your hosting company, or contact Akismet.

UPDATING WORDPRESS SO YOU DON'T LOSE EVERYTHING

It's refreshingly simple to update WordPress. When an update is available, you get a message like this one when you log in to your Dashboard.

If you are a risk taker or your blog is new, you could try updating WordPress without backing up your blog, but you'll probably want to make a regular habit of either manually backing up your blog or using one of the automatic blog backup services. Sometimes when you update systems like WordPress, you lose your data or something goes wrong.

When you click on the Please Update Now link, you get a message like the following, and the Backup Your Database and Files link leads you to information like the kind found in the next section in the book, on backing up WordPress.

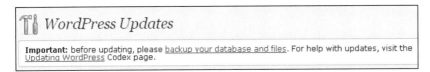

WordPress Updates

Important: before updating, please backup your database and files. For help with updates, visit the Updating WordPress Codex page.

When you're ready to update WordPress, hold your breath, cross your fingers, and click the Update Automatically button.

An updated version of WordPress is available.

You can update to WordPress 3.1.2 automatically or download the package and install it manually:

Update Automatically   Download 3.1.2

(If the update doesn't work, your hosting company might not support the automatic updating feature; HostGator.com seems to support it, so you could always start an account there.)

You'll get an update screen, which hopefully will result in a success message.

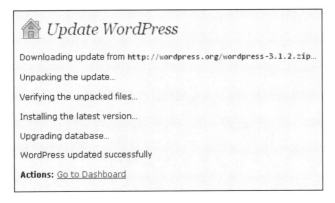

Update WordPress

Downloading update from http://wordpress.org/wordpress-3.1.2.zip...

Unpacking the update...

Verifying the unpacked files...

Installing the latest version...

Upgrading database...

WordPress updated successfully

Actions: Go to Dashboard

Ideally, that's all it takes! And then you can go back to bloggery.

BACKING UP WORDPRESS

Backing up WordPress is a really good idea. See http://codex.wordpress.org/WordPress_Backups.

There are a number of advanced options, but you'll probably want to click the Automated Solutions link.

There are a variety of options; some are free, others not. If you don't mind spending a little money, you might like to investigate the first one, Automatic WordPress Backup, which has the advantage of automatically backing things up.

Automatic Backups

Various plugins exist to take automatic scheduled backups of your WordPress database. This helps to manage your backup collection easily. You can find automatic backup plugins in the Plugin Browser, and some are listed here.

- Automatic WordPress Backup - Automatically backup entire site to Amazon S3.
- BackupWordPress - Back up database as well as files
- WordPress DBManager - Supports automatic scheduling of backing up and optimizing of database
- XCloner - Automatically backup entire wordpress and restore it anywhere.
- WP-DB-Backup Plugin - Email, Save to Server, and Auto-Scheduling
- myRepono WordPress Backup Plugin - Remote and fully automated WordPress, website and database backup.

You can also reach the first link shown in the graphic at http://wordpress.org/extend/plugins/automatic-wordpress-backup/.

For our purposes, we'll look at what it's like to try the second option in the list, which has a manual option and is free. Welcome to the world of installing a WordPress plugin!

INSTALLING A PLUGIN: BACKUPWORDPRESS

In this section, we look at a plugin that can help you back up WordPress: http://wordpress.org/extend/plugins/backupwordpress/.

To get started, click the Download button on the right (see Figure 6.4).

You end up with a .zip file that you should download to your computer. (Don't click on it.)

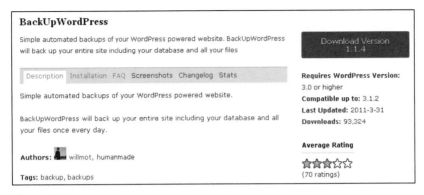

Figure 6.4
The BackUpWordPress plugin.

Then, in your WordPress Dashboard, click the Plugins link.

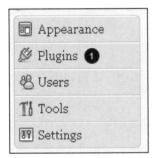

On the Plugins screen, click the Add New button.

And then click the Upload link.

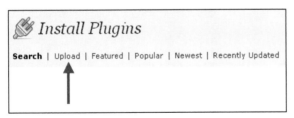

Click the Browse button.

Locate your file in the browse window, double-click on the file, and when you're back on the WordPress screen, click the Install Now button.

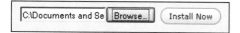

You get a status message that hopefully will result in a success message. Then you can click on the Activate Plugin link.

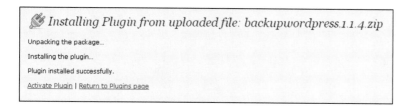

After activating, you *might* get this message. If you really want to dig deep, Google `WordPress Minify`. Otherwise, you can ignore the Minify part. But I didn't say that, and we didn't have this conversation.

What you can do is click the Empty the Page Cache button, which helps WordPress catch up a bit with what you're doing.

empty the page cache

You should get a confirmation message.

Page cache successfully emptied.

Then you can find the BackUpWordPress plugin on your Plugins page.

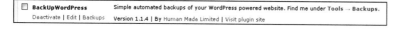

To get to the Backup tool, try clicking on the Tools icon on your Dashboard.

And then click on the Backups link.

If you want to dig deep, you can learn how to use the web-based Control Panel of your hosting account, learn how to use the File Manager, and regularly download the automated backups.

Or you can just click the Back Up Now button.

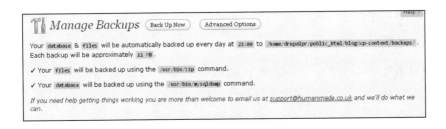

Depending on how much bloggery you've been up to, the system will chomp on it a bit, and then there will be a Download link.

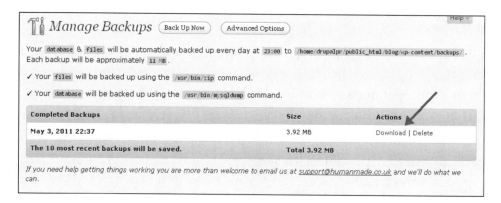

You can download a file that is a backup of your blog, which theoretically allows you to restore it in the event of a catastrophic failure or a hacker attack of some kind.

If you ever need to restore a backup, try visiting http://codex.wordpress.org/ WordPress_Backups and looking in the Manual Backup area for the Restoring link.

You might also want to investigate the WordPress Support Forum link.

Below are instructions to back up your WordPress Site and your WordPress Database as well as resources for automatic WordPress back up. In addition, support is provided online at the WordPress Support Forum to help you through the process.

Or just visit www.wordpress.org and click on the Forums tab.

Another option is to contact the support for your hosting company.

Best wishes, and may you never have to restore a backup!

BLOGBOOKER

it of fun. You've eaten your vegetables by reading this entire ...ying everything. Now you're ready for dessert: exploring Blog-...! It's cool.

BlogBooker allows you to create an ebook of your blog, which can be a nice way of backing things up. It can also be a nice way of sending a PDF of your blog to someone or printing it out as a holiday, birthday, or anniversary present or just keeping it around for future generations.

In fact, I highly encourage your getting a Gmail account. Use it as your permanent, primary email address (it has a lot of advantages, including many free integrated tools), and explore the Calendar feature. Then set yourself a yearly reminder to make a BlogBooker of your blog (see http://mail.google.com).

To get started, visit www.blogbooker.com/ and click on the WordPress link (see Figure 6.5).

Figure 6.5
The BlogBooker site.

Next, you need to learn how to jump through a couple of hoops.

First, you need to export your WordPress blog as an XML file. The How to Export Your Blog as XML link leads to a helpful tutorial. You basically go into the Tools area in your WordPress Dashboard and click Export.

Then you click the Download Export File button.

Next, you download the file, and on the BlogBooker > WordPress page, you click the Browse button, locate your file in the Browse window, and double-click on it.

The next step is to paste the address for your blog into the Blog URL field.

Your Blog URL is whatever your hosted blog address is. Click Create your BlogBook.

You get a status message and a time estimate based on how much you have on your blog.

Then you get a Donate button and a link to your downloadable PDF file (see Figure 6.6).

Your Blog in PDF Book.
(80.02 KB)

Figure 6.6
The download page, after the blog has processed.

I recommend right-clicking and choosing something like Save Link As (Windows) or Ctrl-clicking and choosing Download to Disk (Mac).

But you can also just click on the link. If all goes well, a PDF file downloads and automatically opens. Depending on your browser and computer settings, the PDF downloads somewhere on your computer. But within the Adobe Reader application, you should be able to click on the disk icon to save a copy somewhere specific.

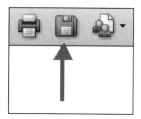

The PDF format is nice. It gathers all your posts in a single file, suitable for printing and emailing.

Woohoo!

CONCLUSION

Dear Reader,

Congratulations! You've made it past the Bridge of Death, and you've successfully avoided the Gorge of Eternal Peril! May your comment spam be little, may you never have need of restoring your backups, and may your in-person road trip to the Spam Museum in Austin, Minnesota, be enjoyable and surreal. Please email me pictures if you go: tekelsey@gmail.com.

In the next chapter, we look at getting a blog going. Forgive me for starting with spam. I figured I might as well get it out of the way and increase the chances of its being read by putting it earlier in the book rather than later!

Regards,

Todd

CHAPTER 7

EASY LAUNCH: GETTING YOUR BLOG GOING

In This Chapter:

- Tweaking a Theme
- Setting Up the Basic Configuration
- Making a Post

The purpose of this chapter is to review some of the basics of getting a blog going. You can go many directions in customizing your blog, and you may find as time goes on that you'll want to come back to some of the many features within WordPress. If you feel best about tweaking the visual design of your blog before you share it with the world, that's one way to go. Another is just to cover the basics of your visual layout and configuration and just start posting!

As you learn about some of the features of WordPress, one thing that can be helpful is to look at other WordPress blogs to see the kinds of things that people are doing with them. For example, http://wordpress.org/showcase has a number of WordPress blogs (see Figure 7.1), including various categories. (And remember that you can always come back and submit *your* blog!)

Visiting a few other blogs may give you ideas, and if the creators of the blogs include their contact information, you might even get a response with a short, polite inquiry about how they achieved a particular feature on their site.

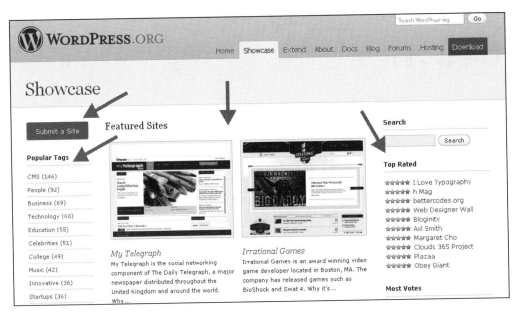

Figure 7.1
Some things to explore on WordPress.org/showcase.

Also, keep your eyes peeled for Chapter 15, "A Few Sample Blogs," where there are some sample blogs and a few thoughts about each person's experience in using WordPress.

Tweaking a Theme

A *theme* in WordPress is a built-in template that organizes the look and feel of your blog. In this section, we look at a couple of basic tweaks you can make to the built-in theme. (And in Chapter 10, "Easy Expansion: Themes and Pages," we look at how to install additional themes.)

To get started, click the Appearance button in your Dashboard.

The Appearance area has a few different options; we'll start with the Themes option and look at a couple of others. Try selecting the Themes link.

There are two tabs in the Themes area: Manage Themes, and Install Themes. Manage Themes allows you to tweak themes that are already installed, and Install Themes allows you to install new ones. (We'll look at installing new themes in Chapter 10.) Under the Manage Themes tab, try clicking on the Header link (see Figure 7.2).

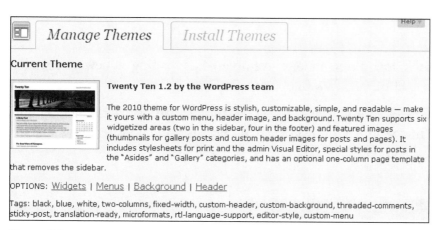

Figure 7.2
The Manage Themes tab.

The Header feature allows you to adjust what displays at the top of your blog. The current theme that is built in to WordPress at the time of writing includes a layout with a long horizontal image, 940 × 198 pixels. There are some additional preformatted images you can try, and you can upload a custom image (see Figure 7.3). You can preformat an image so that it is 940 × 198 pixels, or you can just use the built-in tool and crop a picture when you upload it in WordPress; we'll look at how to do this.

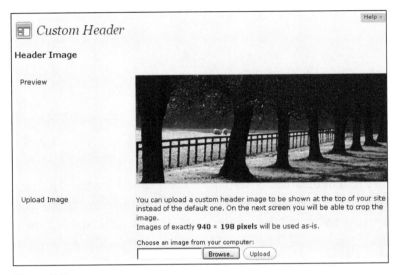

Figure 7.3
Custom Header > Uploading an image.

If you want to follow along in our example of uploading a new image, try searching for a picture on www.publicdomainpictures.net.

When you find a picture you like, to "grab" the picture, try right-clicking and choosing Save Image As (Windows), or Ctrl-clicking and choosing Download to Disk (Mac). See Figure 7.4.

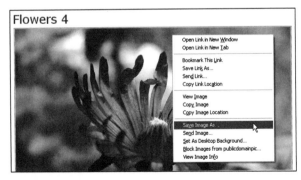

Figure 7.4
Right-clicking (Windows) or Ctrl-clicking (Mac) on an image to download.

Save the image in a location where you can find it. Back in the WordPress Dashboard, in the Custom Header screen, click on the Browse button, locate the image file on your computer, double-click on it, and then click on the Upload button.

Depending on the dimensions of your picture, WordPress allows you to crop it. You can click and drag the little selection squares to adjust the cropping area if you like (see Figure 7.5).

Figure 7.5
Cropping an image.

Or you may just find it easier to decide what part of the picture to keep by rolling over the central area with the mouse pointer, clicking, and dragging the horizontal cropping rectangle to the desired spot on your picture.

The best way to get a feel for cropping is just to try it. When you're done, click Crop and Publish.

Crop and Publish

You will theoretically get a confirmation message like the following image. Unless you want to lose your Dashboard screen, you might like to right-click (Windows) or Ctrl-click (Mac) and open the link in a new tab to make it easier to get back to your Dashboard.

Then you should see something like the following image (see Figure 7.6), with your newly minted header image. One thing you might like to do for variety is to try uploading new images on a regular basis.

Figure 7.6
Blog with custom header image.

Next we'll take a look at how to choose one of the preinstalled header images. To start, go to Appearance > Header in your Dashboard.

Then click on one of the radio buttons to the left of one of the horizontal "default" images (see Figure 7.7).

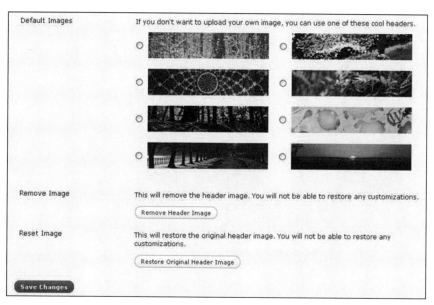

Figure 7.7
Some additional header images and options.

Click the Save Changes button, and you see the new image at the top of your blog.

SETTING UP THE BASIC CONFIGURATION

In this section, we look at some of the basic settings you might like to try changing as you get your blog going. WordPress has *a lot* of options, but don't feel like you need to use every one of them. Many people use only a few of them. What happens over time is that if you get into blogging more, you're more likely to come back and to tweak some of the fine points.

To get started, click the Settings link.

There's a page full of general settings, but you might at least want to get familiar with how to adjust the Site Title and Tagline.

To adjust them, just enter in new text.

And when you're done, click the Save Changes button.

Your changes are reflected on the blog (see Figure 7.8).

Figure 7.8
New blog title and tagline.

Another place where you can make basic adjustments is in the Widgets area. Try clicking on Appearance > Widgets.

The Widgets area is basically a drag-and-drop way to add and rearrange new features.

The area on the right, marked Primary Widget Area, has a list of what is currently installed (see Figure 7.9). You can rearrange the widgets there or drag new ones over from the left. If you feel like going for it, by all means, drag and drop, and then go look at your blog. (You may need to click the Refresh button on your browser.)

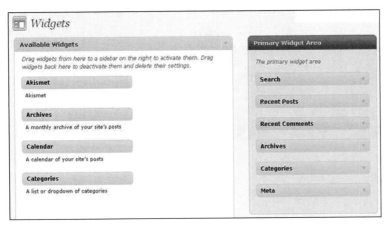

Figure 7.9
Draggable widgets.

The widgets in the Primary Widgets Area correspond to the rightmost panel on your new blog.

So, for example, if you want to try rearranging things, try rolling over one of the widgets, such as the Categories widget, until you get a four-headed mouse pointer.

Then drag it into a different place, such as below the Search widget.

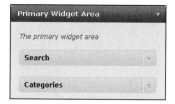

Next, go back and look at your blog. If you repositioned the Categories widget underneath Search, back in your Dashboard, it should look something like this on your blog. (You might need to click Refresh on the browser for the changes to be reflected on your blog page.)

In addition to repositioning widgets, you can change settings on them. For example, in the Primary Widgets Area, try clicking on the downward-facing triangle at the right side of the Categories widget.

It expands and shows a few options.

For example, instead of displaying the word *Categories* at the top of this widget, you can enter in a new title. (The Categories widget displays/organizes your posts by categories; see Chapter 8, "Easy Content: Categories and SEO.")

When you're done, click the Save button. When you go back to your blog and click Refresh, you should see the title of the widget change.

Making a Post

And now, a toast to posts, which are the bread and butter of blogging!

To make a post, in your Dashboard, just click the New Post button. (Click on the left side; the right side has a number of options that aren't important at this stage.)

The new post window appears.

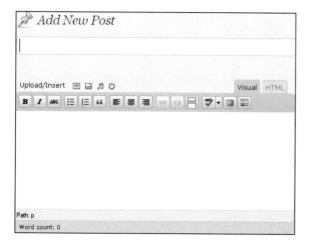

You can enter a title in the top field and then use the formatting buttons at the top of the text area, which are similar to a word processing program.

If you want to insert/upload an image, begin by placing the cursor on another line. (For example, press Enter a few times.)

Then click the leftmost icon by Upload/Insert.

Next, click the Select Files button.

Then locate an image on your computer and double-click on it. For trying things out, you might like to visit www.publicdomainpictures.net, search for a picture of a varmint, and right-click > Save Image As (Windows) or Ctrl-click > Download to Disk (Mac) to save it to your computer.

After you've uploaded the image, scroll down in the WordPress image window and click the Insert into Post button.

Insert into Post

A preview of the image should appear.

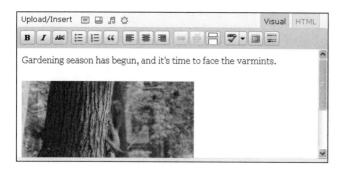

As you compose posts, you have a number of options. If you are just starting a post, and you want to come back and work on it later, you can click Save Draft. You can click Preview to see what it looks like. Generally speaking, though, you just click the Publish button.

Then you should see a confirmation message at the top of your Dashboard. If you want to use the View Post link, try right-clicking > Open New Tab (Windows) or Ctrl-clicking > Open New Tab (Mac).

Once you've made posts, you can always come back and change them. To access posts, click the Posts button in your Dashboard.

A list of posts appears. The easiest way to make a change to a post is just to click on its title.

CONCLUSION

Dear Reader,

Congratulations on making it through a whirlwind tour of some blogging basics! We reviewed how to tweak some theme settings, engaged in some basic configuration, and made a basic post. Blogging can be as simple as you like it.

Some people do their basic configuration, and (gasp) never tweak their blog again! And that's fine and dandy. But other bloggers like to customize things, add pages (see Chapter 10), and engage in as much promotion and tweaking as possible. There's no right or wrong.

The rest of this book takes a closer look at some of the options. As you've seen, the WordPress Dashboard has a lot of options; the best advice I have, especially if you're a beginner, and especially if you feel intimidate at all, is to try clicking on things that seem fun!

Regards,

Todd

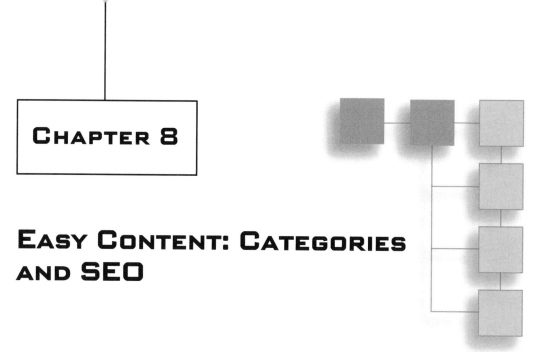

CHAPTER 8

EASY CONTENT: CATEGORIES AND SEO

In This Chapter:

- Categories
- SEO
- Search-Engine-Friendly URLs
- WordPress Versus Facebook Notes: SEO?

The purpose of this chapter is to explore a couple of additional ways you can work with content in your blog.

The Categories feature can help you arrange blog posts in ways that make it easier for visitors to find them. As the blog posts accumulate while you're blogging, you can help generate interest in the blog by making it usable. Part of the principle of usability is to make it as easy as possible for people to find things. So thinking about what kind of category a post might fit into, and getting into the habit of categorizing as you post, can be a helpful blogging technique.

Search engine optimization (SEO) is another area that can be helpful to learn about; it's part of making your blog available to readers. There are a couple of things you can do to help your posts show up in search engine results (such as if someone is searching for peoples' thoughts or articles on a particular topic). In fact, a popular plugin for WordPress can contribute to this effort. Entire books have been written just on the topic of SEO, but we'll just scratch the surface and give a few pointers for more sources of information.

CATEGORIES

To start exploring Categories, log in to your Dashboard, click the Posts button, and then click the Categories link.

The Categories page appears. Try entering a name for a new category.

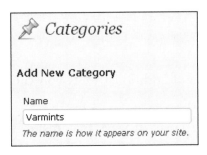

There's additional information you can add, such a description, now or later.

The easiest way to think of categories is like a table of contents; when people are browsing your blog, the categories help them find what they're interested in. You don't have to define all the categories ahead of time; they might emerge as you write about different topics. But you might like to start out with some general categories.

When you're ready, click the Add New Category button.

Your category appears on the right side of the screen, and it indicates how many posts you have that are not categorized.

Name	Description	Slug	Posts
Varmints		varmints	0
Uncategorized		uncategorized	2
Name	Description	Slug	Posts

You can also have subcategories, which can be a helpful way of going from the general high-level categories you might add when you start your blog, toward more specific categories as time goes on.

To create a subcategory, you create a new category and then give it a parent—choosing what the new category will fall under.

For example, enter a new category name, and then choose a parent category in the Parent drop-down menu, as shown in Figure 8.1. (You must have a category created before it will appear there, such as the one we created earlier.)

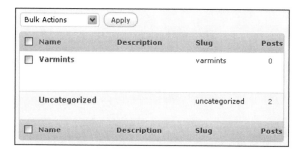

Add New Category

Name

Raccoons

The name is how it appears on your site.

Slug

The "slug" is the URL-friendly version of the name. It is usually all lowercase and contains only letters, numbers, and hyphens.

Parent

None

| None |
| Varmints |
| Uncategorized |

tags, can have a ...ht have a Jazz category, ...ve children categories for Bebop and Big Band. Totally optional.

Figure 8.1
Choosing a parent.

Then click the Add New Category button.

Your subcategory appears in the category list, and it is indented. For example, in the next image, Raccoons is a subcategory of Varmints.

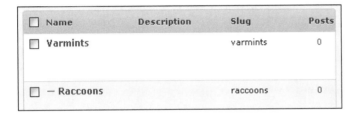

Another thing that's helpful to note as you're working with categories is that when you roll over the category name in the list, options appear, such as Delete.

Categorizing a Post

Now that you've created some categories, it's time to categorize a post!

To start, click the New Post button.

Then create a post as you normally would, and notice the Categories panel in the lower-right corner (see Figure 8.2).

Figure 8.2
Categories panel.

To categorize the post, just click the check box next to the category or categories you'd like to associate the post with.

When you're done, click the Publish button.

Then on your blog, you should see your categories appear. In my case (see previous chapters), I changed the way the Categories panel appears so that it says Table of Contents (see Figure 8.3).

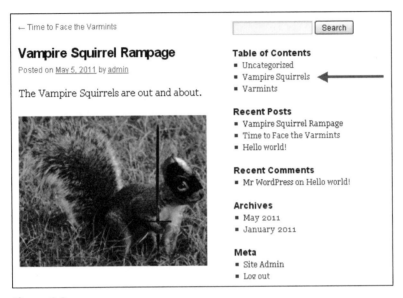

Figure 8.3
The newly minted category links appearing on the blog.

Categorizing the Uncategorized Posts

If you created some posts before getting into categories, you might notice that one of the categories is Uncategorized.

Table of Contents
- Uncategorized
- Vampire Squirrels
- Varmints

Try clicking on that link to see uncategorized posts.

If you'd like to put one of the uncategorized posts in a category, one way to do it is to click the Edit link under a post. (It appears to you when you visit your blog and are logged in, as shown in Figure 8.4.)

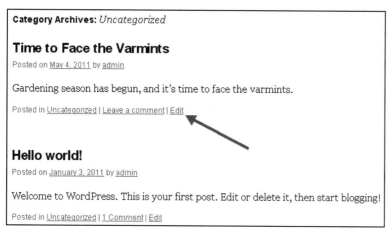

Figure 8.4
Clicking the Edit link at the bottom of a post.

When you access the post, if you look down in the Categories panel, you'll see that the Uncategorized check box is selected. So you can uncheck the Uncategorized option, and then click in the check box of the category or categories you'd like to associate the post with.

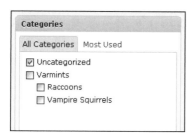

When you're done, click the Update button.

SEO

In this section, we look at a plugin that can be helpful for getting your blog posts to show up in search engine results. Search engines like Google basically "crawl" the web. There are a few tweaks you can make to increase the likelihood that a person will wander across your blog or find a post if they're looking for information on a particular topic. It's more or less a free form of advertising.

To get going, we'll install a popular plugin for WordPress called All in One SEO.

First, click the Plugins button in the Dashboard.

Then click the Add New button.

Adding new plugins in WordPress is pretty easy, and it's nice that you can search for ones right from within WordPress. For example, try entering in all in one seo, and click the Search Plugins button.

Then scroll down until you find All in One SEO Pack, and click the Install Now link. (The version number, such as 1.6.13.2 in the next graphic, might be different when you visit. That's okay.)

You might get a message like this. Just click OK.

Hopefully everything will go all right, you'll get a confirmation message, and you can click the Activate Plugin link.

Then you might get an alarming bright red message saying that All in One SEO Pack needs to be configured. Click on The Admin Page link within that message.

You can also get to the All in One SEO admin page by clicking on Settings > All in One SEO in your Dashboard.

There's a lot of information on the Settings page; at some point you might like to enter your email address to get the free ebook on SEO tips.

Otherwise, this is the section that you'll want to pay the most attention to (see Figure 8.5).

To start, click the Enabled radio button.

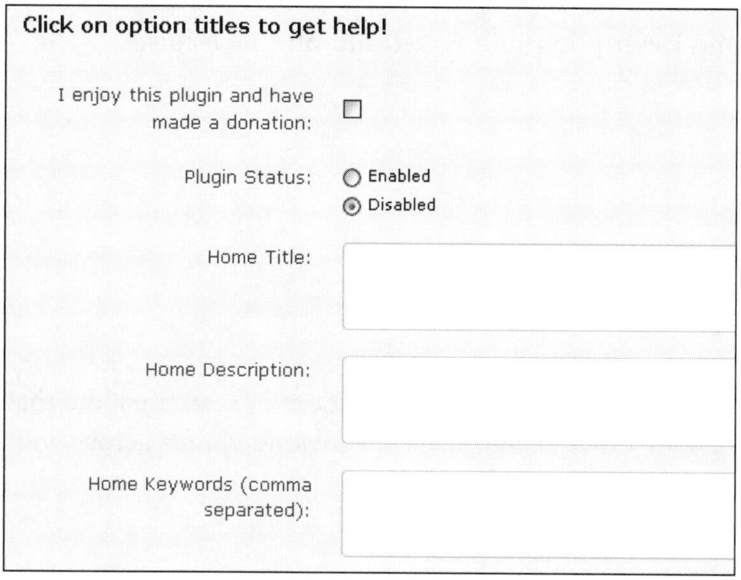

Click on option titles to get help!

I enjoy this plugin and have
made a donation: ☐

Plugin Status: ◯ Enabled
                 ◉ Disabled

Home Title:

Home Description:

Home Keywords (comma
separated):

Figure 8.5
Places to enter in SEO-related information.

Then click on the Home Title link.

This action activates some information. You can just enter the title of your blog
here.

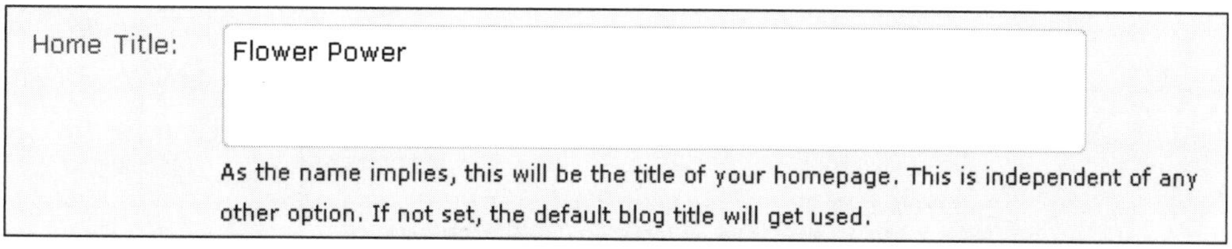

Home Title: Flower Power

As the name implies, this will be the title of your homepage. This is independent of any
other option. If not set, the default blog title will get used.

Similarly, click the Home Description link to get info on this feature.

The Home Description is information that you provide to a search engine that will show up on a Google or other search page if someone comes across your blog. Enter a short description of your blog.

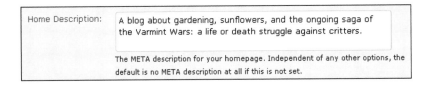

Next, click on Home Keywords.

These keywords are words or phrases that people would type in if they wanted to come across your blog. So if you want your blog to appear in Google search results, when people type in the word gardening, you can enter it as a keyword.

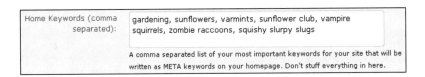

Then, when you're done, click Update Options.

Keep in mind that there's an entire art focused on getting your website or blog to appear in search results; a lot of other people are also hoping to get as high as they can in the results (that is, to be in the first set of pages when someone types in a given word or phrase). So just entering these settings doesn't *guarantee* anything, but it certainly helps. Overall, one of the biggest impacts on search rank is the quality and relevance of your content. That is, when you write something that is interesting, relevant, entertaining, or helpful, people are more likely to share it with someone else or come back and visit your blog again. And Google is out there calculating all the time, so when more people visit your blog or post a link to your blog, Google is keeping track and will boost your rank in search engine results. That, in a nutshell, is SEO.

If you want to get deeper into SEO, there's an ebook titled *SEOBook* by Aaron Wall that has become a classic. Another good one to investigate is a book called *SEO Made Simple*.

SEO for Writing Posts

When you have the All in One SEO plugin installed, you can create the "global settings" for your overall blog, as we just did in the previous section. You can also tweak each post as you create it.

To practice, click the New Post button.

Then create a post as you normally would, and try to get in the habit of doing the following, shown in Figure 8.6:

- Categorizing it
- Doing SEO

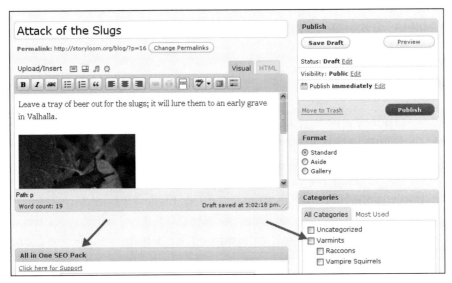

Figure 8.6
Getting in the habit of categorizing and entering in SEO info.

To do SEO for your post, take a look at the All in One SEO panel, as shown in Figure 8.7.

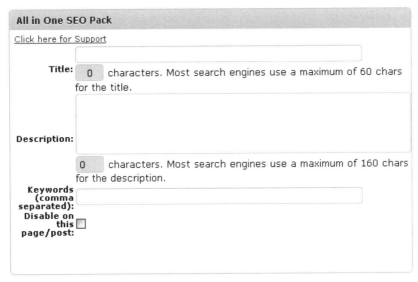

Figure 8.7
Entering in SEO-friendly info.

The All in One SEO panel basically allows you to enter some simple information for each post that helps the post appear in search engine results. Entering the SEO info takes a moment or two, but it can help in the long run.

As you type in a title and description, you get a running count of how many characters are used. For example, in the next image, the title is 19 characters.

Note

Be aware that spaces are counted toward the number of characters.

The description is 98 characters.

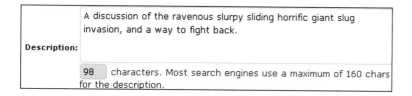

For those of you who see yourself wanting to promote your blog on social media, such as Facebook or Twitter, you might like to keep a copy of the description. It might provide a convenient set of text for a Facebook or Twitter post.

Next, enter some keywords for the post that represent terms people might type in if they are interested in the topic.

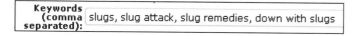

When you're ready, click the Publish button to publish your post.

You can also come back and edit posts and add the SEO information; then you would click the Update button.

Getting Fancy Shmancy with the Code

If you want to get fancy shmancy and go behind the scenes and see the impact of the SEO tweaks on your blog, try visiting the home page of your blog, and then click on the title of one of your blog posts (see Figure 8.8).

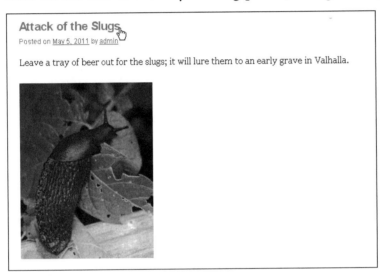

Figure 8.8
Accessing a post.

This action takes you from your general blog to a link that is specific to your post.

Next, depending on your browser (I recommend Firefox), find the feature that allows you to view the source. In Firefox, click View > Page Source.

What this technique allows you to do is see the HTML code for any given web page you visit. WordPress is a content management system, and it takes a lot of the work out of making a website. It used to be that to get anything on the web, you needed to know HTML, and you had to manually put together and upload the code anytime you wanted to add something to your web page. It can still help to learn a bit of HTML, but content management systems can make life a lot easier.

In the case of SEO, what Google is doing is crawling the code of your website. Technically, what your SEO efforts do is leave little bits of code for Google to chew on. If you were manually working on a web page, what you would need to do for SEO is include some "meta" code.

So when you view the source, if you look in the code, you see something like this, which corresponds to the information you entered.

```
<!-- All in One SEO Pack 1.6.13.2 by Michael Torbert of Semper Fi Web Design[78,119] -->
<meta name="description" content="A discussion of the ravenous slurpy sliding horrific giant slug invasion, and a way to fight back." />
<meta name="keywords" content="slugs, slug attack, slug remedies, down with slugs" />
<link rel="canonical" href="http://storyloom.org/blog/?p=16" />
<!-- /all in one seo pack -->
```

Congratulations! You've hacked into the code in a manner of speaking!

If you're interested in learning more about the All in One SEO plugin, try visiting www.wpbeginner.com/plugins/users-guide-for-all-in-one-seo-pack/.

Or just visit http://tinyurl.com/seouserguide, which leads to the same place.

What I just provided was a short URL (uniform resource locator) to the long link, which can be a helpful technique when sharing links on Facebook or Twitter for your blog. If you want to try making a really long link a lot shorter, visit sites like http://is.gd or http://bit.ly, and copy in a link for your blog post. I like tinyurl.com, because you can enter a custom alias. For example, for the earlier link, I pasted the long link—wpbeginner.com blah blah blah really long link—into tinyurl.com and chose a custom alias of seouserguide.

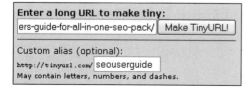

And this resulted in http://tinyurl.com/seouserguide.

Try it. Making postings with limited character lengths can come in handy.

Search-Engine-Friendly URLs

Another thing that can be helpful to tweak in WordPress is the way that links (also known as URLs) display.

For example, without changing settings, the link to your post might appear something like this:

http://storyloom.org/blog/?p=16

But it can make more sense to people and to search engines to have links like this:

http://storyloom.org/blog/2011/05/attack-of-the-slugs/

To tweak this setting, go to Settings > Permalinks in your Dashboard.

Then click the radio button next to the desired format, in the Common Settings area.

Common settings

⦿ Default   http://storyloom.org/blog/?p=123

○ Day and name   http://storyloom.org/blog/2011/05/05/sample-post/

○ Month and name   http://storyloom.org/blog/2011/05/sample-post/

○ Numeric   http://storyloom.org/blog/archives/123

○ Custom Structure

(Personally, I like Month and Name). Then click the Save Changes button.

To see what's going on, click on the title of a blog post to make sure you're on a link for a blog post, not the general blog.

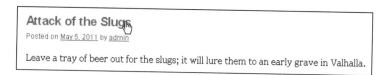

Attack of the Slugs
Posted on May 5, 2011 by admin

Leave a tray of beer out for the slugs; it will lure them to an early grave in Valhalla.

Then, in the address bar of your browser, you should see something like this:

> http://storyloom.org/blog/2011/05/attack-of-the-slugs/

WordPress Versus Facebook Notes: SEO?

As a discussion question, line of research, or experiment, I'd like to take the opportunity to think out loud. One area where having a customized blog might be an advantage over using Notes in Facebook might be in the area of SEO. Depending on the privacy settings, if you make a Note in Facebook, and you type in its exact title, it might show up in search engine results. Here is a poem I wrote, which seems to show up.

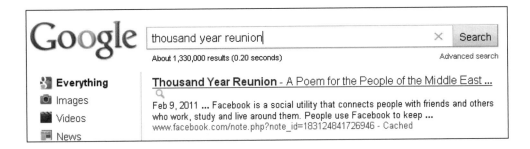

So there's kind of an automated SEO in Facebook Notes, but until/unless Facebook adds it, you don't have the ability in a Facebook Note to add in specific SEO keywords on a per-Note basis.

This seems to lend support for the idea of maintaining a separate blog and then either posting on Facebook/Twitter whenever you make a blog post or importing your blog automatically into your Facebook page so that it becomes a note, as another opportunity for exposure. We'll look at that in Chapter 13, "Promoting on Social Media."

Conclusion

Dear Reader,

Congratulations! You're well on your way toward being an SEO expert. Woohoo!

In this chapter, we've looked at some of the simple techniques you can use to organize and tweak your blog posts so that it's easier for people and for Google to find them.

In the next chapter, we look at one way you can get information on just how many people are visiting your blog and where they're coming from.

Regards,

Todd

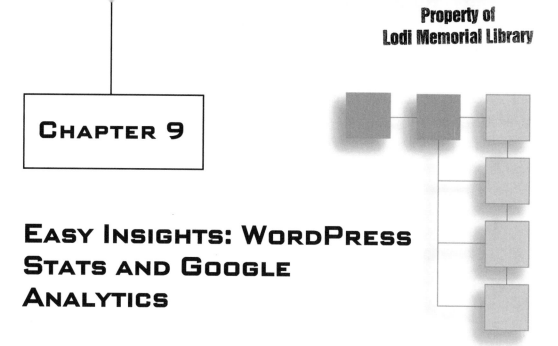

CHAPTER 9

Easy Insights: WordPress Stats and Google Analytics

In This Chapter:

- WordPress.com Stats
- Google Analytics

The purpose of this chapter is to look at a basic set of plugins that can provide insight about how many visits there are to your blog, where people are coming from, and what they click on. Taking a look at this kind of information once in a while can give you valuable insights about your promotion efforts. It can also be helpful to know *where* people are coming from; for example, if you see that you are getting a lot of visitors based on a link from another blog or particular website, you can contact that blog/site and thank it for the link, or you can see if it might like some exposure on your blog. What goes around comes around.

WordPress.com Stats

The WordPress.com stats plugin (stats = statistics) is a good place to start; it's a popular plugin that makes a go of providing the information that is likely to be most relevant to a blogger.

To see basic information about the plugin, visit http://wordpress.org/extend/plugins/stats/.

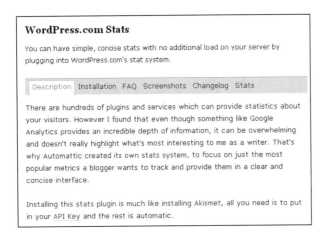

To try it out, visit Plugins > Add New in your Dashboard.

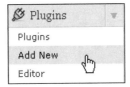

Then type `stats` into the search field and click the Search Plugins button.

Next, click the Install link.

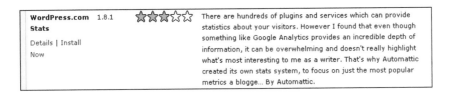

And click the OK button if you get a message like this.

Hopefully you'll get a success confirmation message, and you can then click the Activate Plugin link.

You will be returned to the Plugins page, and you will probably see a "needs attention" message; you can click on the WordPress.com Stats link to do basic configuration.

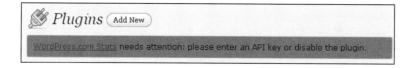

For the stats plugin to work, you need to get a code from a separate website and come back and plug the code in here. When you click on the Get Your Key Here link, I recommend right-clicking (Windows) or Ctrl-clicking (Mac) and opening the link in a new tab.

The WordPress.com Stats Plugin is not working because it needs to be linked to a WordPress.com account.

Enter your WordPress.com API key to link this blog to your WordPress.com account. Be sure to use your own API key! Using any other key will lock you out of your stats. (Get your key here.)

API Key:

Save »

On the next screen, you may get a message like the following, unless you happen to already have a free WordPress.com blog and you are signed into it already.

If you don't already have a WordPress.com account or you're not signed into it, you need to click on the Sign Up link, or you need to log into your WordPress.com blog and come back and visit http://apikey.wordpress.com/ (the equivalent of clicking on the Get Your Key Here link in the previous graphic).

You end up getting a message like the following:

```
Your WordPress.com username is "olpc" and your API key is
    "aas98sddsk8ad9323as"
```

So the idea is that you take the application programming interface (API) key (the letters and numbers between the quotes) and bring it back into WordPress, enter it into the API Key field, and click the Save button.

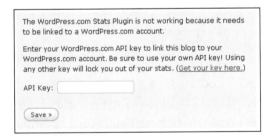

(If you get the API key and then get lost, the way you get back to the WordPress Stats module is Plugins > WordPress.com Stats.)

When you enter the API key and click Save, you get a message like the following, and you can click the Add Blog to WordPress.com button.

Then there will be some additional options. You can click the Save Options button (see Figure 9.1).

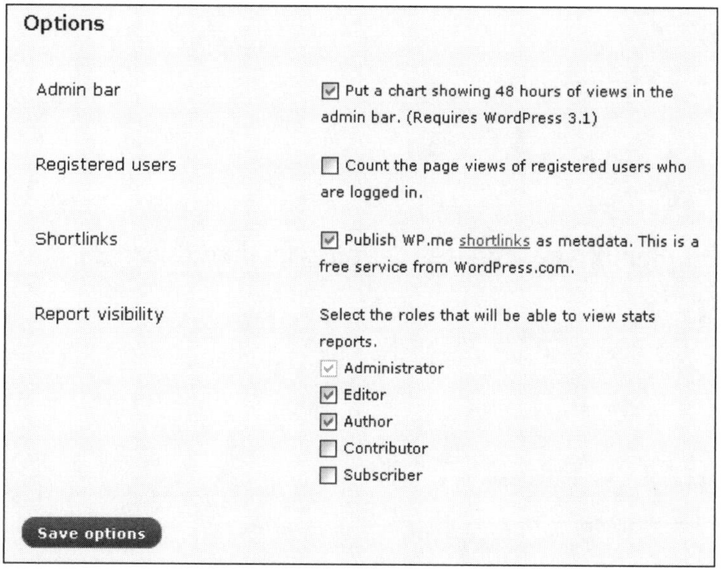

Figure 9.1
Stats options.

If you ever want to come back and adjust settings, you can go to Plugins > WordPress.com Stats.

To access information on site visitors, you can go to Dashboard > Site Stats.

If you've just installed the plugin, you might get a message like this.

Also, you might want to get on Facebook or send a few emails asking people to visit your blog to generate some test clicks; the WordPress.com Stats plugin theoretically doesn't track your own visits to the site. Then wait a half hour and come back and take a look.

You see a graph. If it's the first day of using it, the most you get is a little dot. On the left are numbers that represent the number of visits.

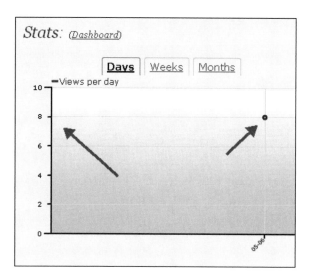

If you scroll down further on the page, depending on what you've posted and what people have clicked on, you might see more information. Consulting this kind of information can give you an idea of what people like, and the overall visits information can give you a sense of trends, such as whether there is an increase in visitors.

There's also a Referrers section, which can provide insight about where people are visiting from. If/when people post a link to your blog from theirs, it shows up as a referrer, and if you made a post on Facebook, it also shows up.

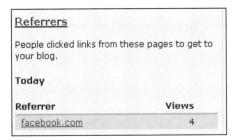

Another way to view stats information is directly on the Dashboard.

There is a little panel you can scroll down to that gives a bird's-eye view of what's going on (see Figure 9.2).

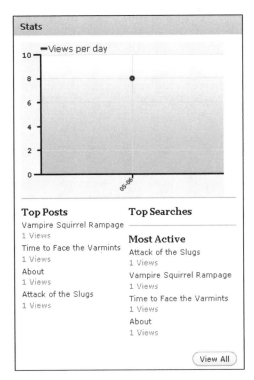

Figure 9.2
Dashboard panel with stats info.

GOOGLE ANALYTICS

WordPress.com stats might be all some bloggers need, but you might also want to explore Google Analytics. It can be a helpful to get more comfortable with Google Analytics, especially if you see yourself wanting to learn more about online advertising or online marketing. Google Analytics is a powerful tool that can provide good information about site visitors; it also has some fun features, such as reports that can show where people are coming from geographically.

Several different plugins allow you to connect Google Analytics; here's the general process:

1. Installing a plugin in WordPress.
2. Starting a Google account. (You can use a non-Gmail address to start a Google account, but I recommend starting a Gmail account because of how helpful Gmail is, including all the free tools you get with it, such as Google Documents.)
3. Activating Google Analytics and getting a code, also known as a *web property ID.*
4. Bringing the code back into WordPress.

One of the Google Analytics WordPress plugins is Google Analyticator. To learn more about it, visit http://wordpress.org/extend/plugins/google-analyticator/.

To get started, go to Plugins > Add New.

Then enter Google Analyticator in the search field, and click Search Plugins.

Next, click Install Now.

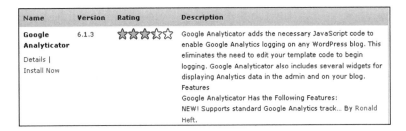

Click OK if you get a message like this.

Hopefully you'll get a success confirmation message, and you can click the Activate Plugin link.

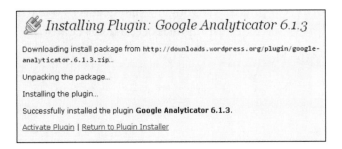

Google Analyticator shows up in the plugins list.

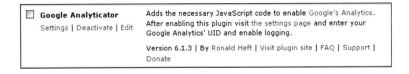

Next, you will: set up a Google Analytics account, get the web property ID/ UID code from Google Analytics, and then come back to WordPress and enter it in.

Step 1, Option 1: Setting Up Google Analytics and Getting a UID

If you don't have a Gmail or Google account, or you do but you've never used Google Analytics before, follow the instructions in this section. If you've used Google Analytics before, skip to the next section, "Step 1, Option 2: Returning to Google Analytics If It's Not Your First Time."

If you don't have a Google account or Gmail account, visit http://mail.google. com, create a Gmail account, and log in.

If you do have a Google/Gmail account, log in to it.

Then, visit www.google.com/analytics/ and click Access Analytics.

If you haven't logged in yet, you're given an opportunity to do so.

Next, click the Sign Up button.

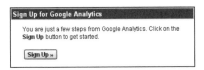

In the New Account Signup area, you need to enter the address for your blog. Google Analytics accounts can be used to track multiple websites and blogs; you can create new website profiles and get new codes to track each site. But starting out, you can enter only a single address. The account name can be whatever you like: your name, your blog's name, whatever.

Then choose the desired country and time zone settings, and click Continue (see Figure 9.3).

Analytics: New Account Signup

General Information > Contact Information > Accept User Agreement > Add Tracking

Please enter the URL of the site you wish to track, and assign a name as it should appear in your Google Analytics reports. If you'd like to track more than one website, you can add more sites once your account has been set up. Learn more.

Website's URL:	http:// ☑ storyloom.org/blog	(e.g. www.mywebsite.com)
Account Name:	Storyloom	
Time zone country or territory:	United States ☑	
Time zone:	(GMT-05:00) Central Time ☑	

Cancel   Continue »

Figure 9.3
Google Analytics signup; you only need one account, which you can use to track multiple websites, through adding more profiles.

Next enter your name and country, and click Continue.

Analytics: New Account Signup

General Information > Contact Information > Accept User Agreement > Add Tracking

Last Name:	Kelsey
First Name:	Todd
Country or territory:	United States ☑

« Back   Continue »

Click the Yes check box, and click Create New Account.

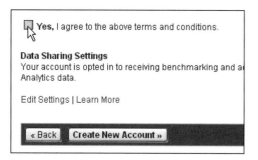

What Google Analytics does is provide a set of tracking codes that can be added to a website to allow tracking; in this case, all we need is a small part of it: the ID, starting with UA.

If you like, you can select and copy this code from this screen, or you can get it from the next screen.

My code, for this specific blog, is UA-23169791-1.

Click the Save and Finish button to wrap things up.

The next screen shows the code again (starting with UA). It might be easier to select and copy it from this screen. You could paste it back into WordPress directly, but it might be helpful to paste it into a text editing document or email to yourself so you can keep track of it.

Step 1, Option 2: Returning to Google Analytics If It's Not Your First Time

(If you've already gotten your Google Analytics code, you can skip ahead to "Step 2: Bringing the Google Analytics Code Back into WordPress.")

If you already have Google Analytics associated with your Gmail/Google account, you might already have a UID for another website or blog. If so, you can add a new Web Profile to your existing Google Analytics account, which gives you a code you can bring back into WordPress.

If you do have an account already, visit http://google.com/analytics.

Then toward the bottom of the screen, click Add Website Profile.

Add Website Profile»
A profile allows you to track a website and/or create different views of the reporting data using filters. Learn more

Enter the address of your blog, choose the time zone settings, and click Finish (see Figure 9.4).

Then you can select and copy the Web Property ID from this screen, or get it from the next screen.

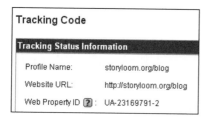

Figure 9.4
Adding a new profile.

(The code in this example, for this specific blog of mine, is UA-23169791-2.)

Tracking Code	
Tracking Status Information	
Profile Name:	storyloom.org/blog
Website URL:	http://storyloom.org/blog
Web Property ID ⑦ :	UA-23169791-2

To wrap things up, click Save and Finish.

You can also get the code from the next screen.

Step 2: Bringing the Google Analytics Code Back into WordPress

Now that you have your code, go back into WordPress and into Google Analyticator and plug in your code.

To get back there, if the screen is not already open, click Plugins.

Find the Google Analyticator plugin, and click the Settings link or The Settings Page link.

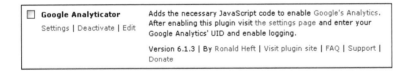

You get a message indicating that the plugin is initially disabled (see Figure 9.5).

First, click the Disabled drop-down menu and switch it to Enabled.

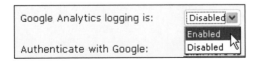

Figure 9.5
Notification that you need to enable.

Next, find the UID section.

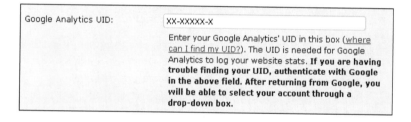

Enter the code.

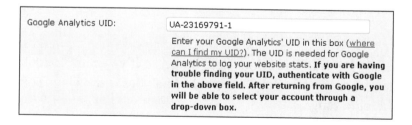

Then scroll down and click Save Changes.

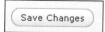

Accessing Google Analytics

One way to check your information on your blog with Google Analytics is to visit Google Analytics.

To try it out, visit www.google.com/analytics.

Keep in mind that the data might not start gathering for as long as a day.

You see something like the following. To get started, click the View Report link (see Figure 9.6).

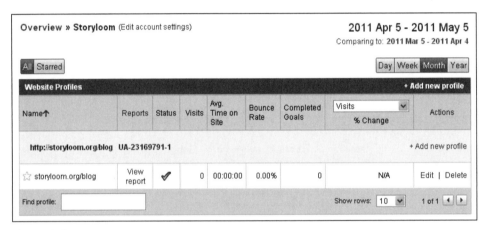

Figure 9.6
High-level view of website profiles in Google Analytics. To dig deeper, click on a profile.

Google Analytics generally looks to a previous date range, so if you want to look at data for a specific day, be aware of what day Google Analytics is showing. You might need to reset the date range.

For example, say it was May 6, and that day's data wasn't showing. You can click on the date range.

And then you can select the date you want.

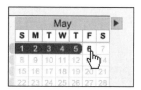

And click Apply.

Generally speaking, you don't necessarily need to adjust date ranges, but if you do have some visits as a result of making a post on Facebook or sending an email, you might need to set the date range to the current day, if it's the first time you're using Google Analytics.

A variety of high-level information displays (see Figure 9.7).

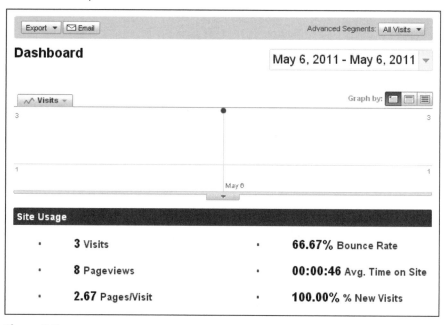

Figure 9.7
High-level information; date range has been adjusted to a single day.

There are also some interesting overview reports. You can click on the View Report links at the bottom of any of them (see Figure 9.8).

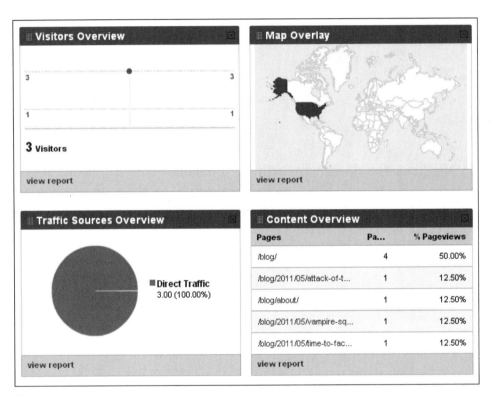

Figure 9.8
Various overviews. Click the View Report links for more info.

Enabling the Dashboard Widget

Google Analyticator has a dashboard widget that allows you to see Google Analytics information from within WordPress. To enable it, visit Settings > Google Analytics.

Then click on the Click Here To Login to Google link. Basically you need to connect WordPress and Google.

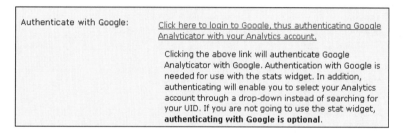

If you're not signed in already, you can enter your Google/Gmail account information.

Then click the Grant Access button.

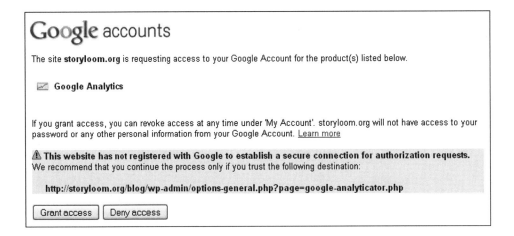

Next, you should see that Google Analyticator is authenticated.

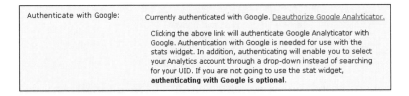

When done, scroll down and click Save Changes.

To access the information, click Dashboard.

Then scroll down until you see a Google Analytics Summary panel. After you've been gathering data for a few days, information shows up here.

```
┌─────────────────────────────────────────┐
│ Google Analytics Summary                 │
├─────────────────────────────────────────┤
│ Visits Over the Past 30 Days             │
│                                          │
│                                          │
│                                          │
│ ──────────────────────────────           │
│ Site Usage                               │
│                                          │
│ Top Pages                                │
│ There is no data for view.               │
│                                          │
│ Top Referrers          Top Searches      │
│ There is no data for view. There is no data for view. │
│                                          │
└─────────────────────────────────────────┘
```

CONCLUSION

Dear Reader,

Welcome to the world of stats and analytics! When I started out with Google Analytics, I felt a bit intimidated, because it's a tool that's evolved to include a lot of information that websites want to keep track of. But after using it a bit, I started to see the value, and the best advice I have for you regarding Google Analytics is this: don't feel like you have to know every function. Just focus on the information that looks most useful and relevant to you.

If you do try Google Analytics, you might like to see where people are coming from, as well as how much time they are spending on your site. When you have a number of articles on the site, you might like to try the technique of learning how to add a link to the end of each blog post, inviting people to visit other blog posts, such as "If you liked this blog post, you might also like to try _____," and include a link to the other post. Then, in Google Analytics, you might like to see if this results in increasing the average time people spend on your site.

I also recommend keeping a regular eye on referrers on either WordPress.com Stats or Google Analytics. Regularly taking a look at where people are coming from can give you an idea of whether people out there are linking to your blog. If they are, you might want to thank them for it or approach them about some kind of partnership.

There's nothing wrong with just going with a simpler stats option like WordPress.com Stats. It provides some good information and is easy to use.

Best wishes!

Regards,

Todd

CHAPTER 10

EASY EXPANSION: THEMES AND PAGES

In This Chapter:

- Adding and Switching Themes
- Adding and Accessing Pages

The purpose of this chapter is to look at how you can further personalize your site by going out and finding different themes to adjust the look and feel. Some people choose one theme and stick with it; other people like to try different themes.

We also take a look at pages in WordPress, a feature that allows you to add more conventional pages to a WordPress site. Blog posts might be added regularly or occasionally and even have categories, whereas pages might represent permanent pages, such as About, Mission, and so on.

ADDING AND SWITCHING THEMES

To explore some of the themes that are out there, click on Appearance in the Dashboard.

Then click the Install Themes tab.

You can search for themes in different ways. If you know the name of one you would like to find, you can enter it in the search box and click Search, or you can click on one of the links at the top to browse.

There's also a Feature Filter, where you can check various features that might be of interest (see Figure 10.1) and then click the Find Themes button.

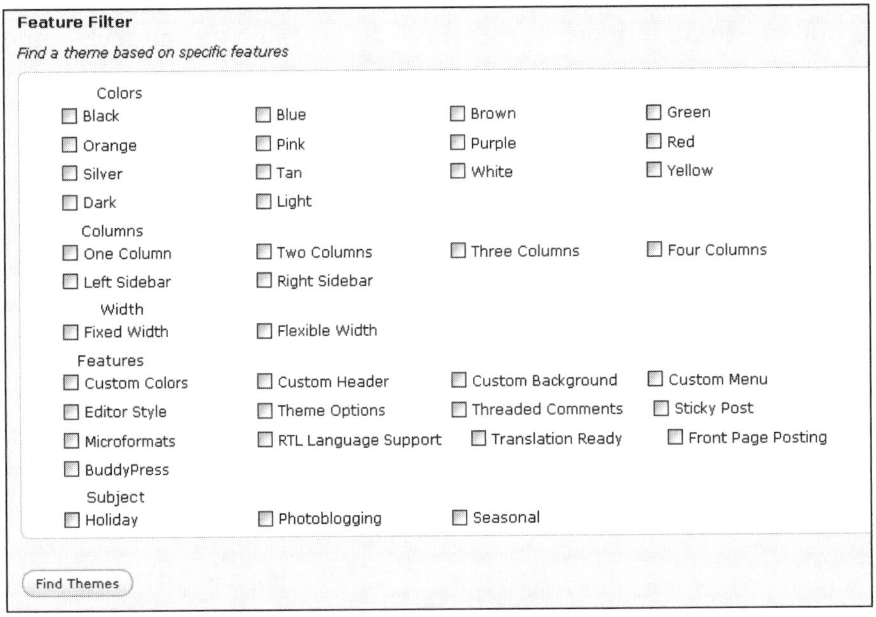

Figure 10.1
The Feature Filter allows you to search based on features you would like in a theme.

To get started, I suggest trying the Featured link at the top.

Search | Upload | Featured | Newest | Recently Updated

Depending on what themes WordPress has featured at the time, you can scroll around and find one that is of interest to you. (If you don't see any of the ones used in these examples when browsing, try the Search feature.)

When you find something that looks interesting, you can try clicking the Preview link (see Figure 10.2).

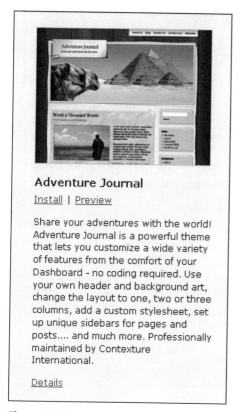

Adventure Journal

Install | Preview

Share your adventures with the world! Adventure Journal is a powerful theme that lets you customize a wide variety of features from the comfort of your Dashboard - no coding required. Use your own header and background art, change the layout to one, two or three columns, add a custom stylesheet, set up unique sidebars for pages and posts.... and much more. Professionally maintained by Contexture International.

Details

Figure 10.2
Browsing themes.

A window pops up that gives you a sense of what the theme would look like, and you might get a scrollbar on the right that you can use to scroll down through and see whatever doesn't fit in the window (see Figure 10.3). When you're done previewing, you can click the little X in the upper-left corner.

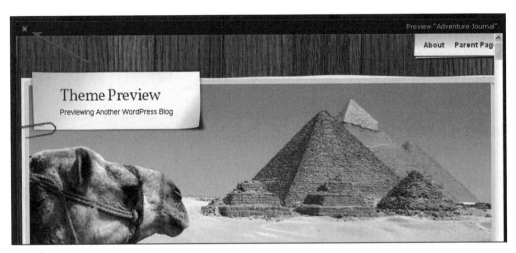

Figure 10.3
A theme preview.

As an example, I suggest browsing in the Featured themes (or searching by name) for the News theme. Then click Install when you're ready.

A window pops up, and you can click Install Now.

Similar to a plugin, a confirmation message appears. When you're ready, you can click the Activate link.

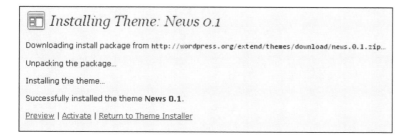

When you install and activate a new theme, it shows up at the top of the list of themes (see Figure 10.4). You might also get a message inviting you to adjust your widget settings.

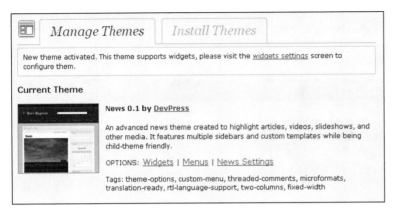

Figure 10.4
A newly activated theme, showing up at the top of the list of themes.

For now, let's just look at your blog (and click the Refresh button if necessary) so we can see the impact of the new theme (see Figure 10.5). It's basically like trying on a new outfit for your blog site; then you can tweak things from there.

Figure 10.5
A new theme can significantly change the look and feel.

To get back and look at adjusting widget settings, visit Appearance > Widgets in the Dashboard.

Basically what happens is that when you install a new theme, you might need to choose custom settings for that theme, such as placing any widgets you want to appear (even if you already did that for another theme). A new theme may carry over some of your old information, or it may not. In my case, I had used the Categories and Archives widget, so I could drag those over.

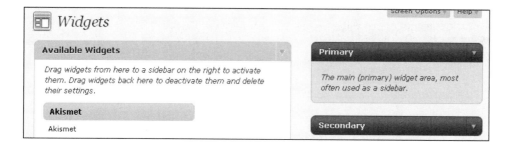

For example, what you do on the widgets screen is scroll down and choose whatever you wanted to drag over and move the mouse pointer over it until it changes into a four-headed mouse pointer.

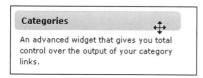

Then you can drag it over and up into the Primary widget area, until a little dotted box appears. Then you can drop it.

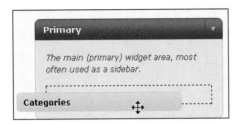

When you drag a widget over, it may expand and offer settings you can change. You can click the downward-facing triangle to collapse it, or you can enter in information and click the Save button.

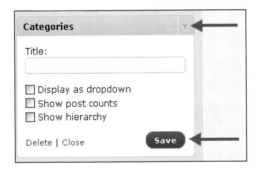

Then, after you adjust your widget settings, they should be reflected on your blog, such as in this case, where Categories now appears on the right (see Figure 10.6).

Then if you want to get back and adjust settings further, you can select Appearance > Themes.

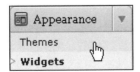

Figure 10.6
Re-adding a widget that was blown out by the new theme.

Your theme shows up under Current Theme. Generally speaking, it's a good idea to explore the links and settings on a theme; for example, this News theme has a link called Menus that can allow you to add some functionality to your site.

The Menus link leads to a custom menu builder (for example, for a conventional drop-down menu that you can add to your blog site for categories of news/information).

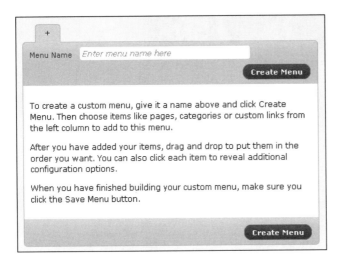

After you get a new theme on your blog, you might very well want to just switch back! To switch between installed themes, select Appearance > Themes.

The last theme you used appears under the list of Available Themes, and you can click the Activate link (see Figure 10.7).

Ah! Back to the old theme. But wait, where did my nice Table of Contents panel go? Well, sometimes when you switch back and forth, you might need to re-create some elements. In this case, it appears that my custom header image of the flower was remembered, but I need to go in and use the widgets feature, drag over Categories, and rename it `Table of Contents` to bring things back to normal (see Figure 10.8).

Figure 10.7
Going under the list of available themes to activate the previous theme.

ADDING AND ACCESSING PAGES

Pages are a nice feature to add conventional static pages to a site (ones that might not change much).

To try adding a page, click on the Pages link in the Dashboard.

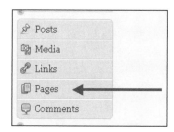

Figure 10.8
Switching back and forth between themes may require rebuilding some widgets, such as the Categories widget, which had been erased for me.

Then click the Add New button.

The Add New Page feature functions similarly to a new blog post; just add in some info (and pictures if you like), and click Publish.

Then you can click the View Page link.

In this particular theme, the page links appear right below a custom header image. The new page that I added, Mission, appears, and a link for it appears at the top (see Figure 10.9).

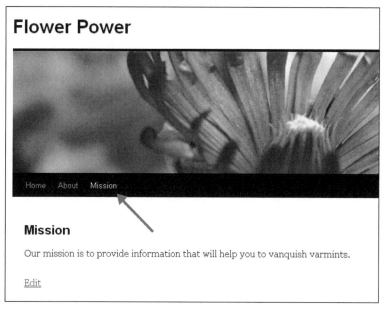

Figure 10.9
A page in WordPress.

Depending on your theme, you might also have a precreated About link, which you can click on.

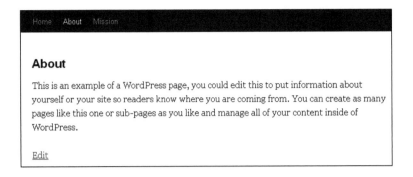

(If you want to change the default text, you can click the Edit link.)

Editing a page is about the same as editing . . . you guessed it . . . a blog post (see Figure 10.10).

Figure 10.10
Editing a page.

Just replace the information as desired and click the Update button (see Figure 10.11). And be sure to add a silly image from www.publicdomainpictures. net—unless it would get you in trouble with your teacher, professor, colleagues, or blog readers!

Figure 10.11
Updating a page.

When you're done, you can click the View Page link.

When you have some pages on your site and want to adjust/edit them, there are a couple ways to do it.

If you're logged into your blog and looking at it, you can click on the admin menu at the top of the screen and select Dashboard.

Or you can get into your Dashboard in the traditional way (for example, http://storyloom.org/blog/wp-admin/index.php or www.yourblogaddress.com/wp-admin/index.php) and click on the Pages link.

Then a list of your pages appears. You can click on the titles of the pages to edit (see Figure 10.12).

Figure 10.12
The list of pages—click on a title to access.

If you have SEO plugins installed (see Chapter 8, "Easy Content: Categories and SEO"), you might like to scroll down when editing a page and enter SEO information (see Figure 10.13).

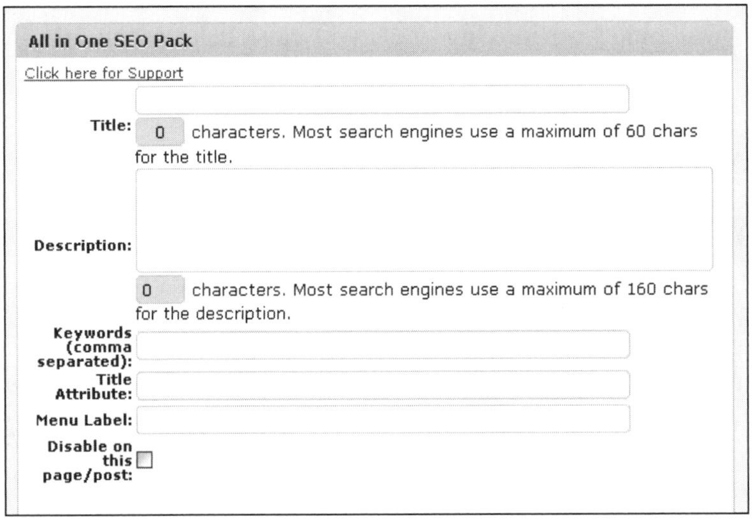

Figure 10.13
Scrolling down to the All in One SEO Pack panel to enter info for a page.

After you make edits to your page, be sure to click the Update button.

When you're looking at your list of pages, another thing you might like to try is rolling over a page title (instead of just clicking it directly), and then clicking on Quick Edit.

Among the things you can do in Quick Edit is assigning your page a number, which affects the order that it appears. A number 0 appears earliest in the list.

Then click the Update button when you're done.

CONCLUSION

Dear Reader,

In this chapter, we've looked at a couple of features that allow you to customize your blog. Some people take their blogs in the direction of a conventional website, with pages, menus, and other traditional features. And others find that all they need to do is just keep posting! If you're interested in advice, I suggest at least adding some information on an About page to describe the blog, give some background, and perhaps even include a welcome message.

In the next chapter, we look at some more ways to have fun, including integrating some content with Facebook and adding a translate function to your blog to make it available in other languages.

Regards,

Todd

CHAPTER 11

EASY EXPANSION: INTEGRATING FACEBOOK AND GTRANSLATE

In This Chapter:

- Facebook Social Plugins
- Changing Widget Settings
- GTranslate
- Share on Facebook

The purpose of this chapter is to explore a couple of fun things you can add to your WordPress blog. They require a little tweaking but can add some extra spice and liven things up. There are a few ways that you can connect Facebook to your blog. Facebook has a feature called social plugins, where you can take a bit of code, put it on your website/blog, and add things such as a Like button. (A Like button provides Facebook members with an easy way for your friends to tell you that they like your site/blog.) You can also integrate other kinds of Facebook content, and with the growth of Facebook, I think that some kind of connection between your site and Facebook is worth thinking about. We'll scratch the surface, and if it looks interesting, I'll encourage you to jump in!

GTranslate is a fun plugin using Google Translate that allows your blog to be available in other languages. There are limits to how much meaning you can get across with computer translation (human translation is significantly better), but Google translation is getting better all the time, and "something" may be better than nothing. If you tried the Google Analytics plugin and dig into Google Analytics in the Visitors information, you can look at where people are coming from and even what language they speak. Don't be surprised if your blog at some point includes people who speak other languages.

Note

> You might have a better experience with Firefox than with Chrome; it's possible for plugins to conflict with each other or have issues when a new version of a browser comes out. The best approach is to try it and see if it will work, and then either wait for a new version of a plugin (or browser) or try again.

FACEBOOK SOCIAL PLUGINS

First, let's look at some things you can add from Facebook. (Don't worry if you're not on Facebook. If you would like a free introduction, see the free sample edition of *Social Networking Spaces* at http://tinyurl.com/snspaces-sed.)

There are two general ways to go when connecting to Facebook with social plugins: getting the code from Facebook and manually bringing it into your site, or using a WordPress plugin to make things easier. We'll do the latter. (But if you want to geek out, or if you're in a class and would like to scratch the surface of the code, see http://developers.facebook.com/docs/plugins/.)

To get started, visit Plugins in your WordPress Dashboard.

Then click the Add New button.

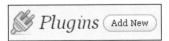

And in the Search box, type in `Facebook Social Plugins`, and click the Search Plugins button.

A list of WordPress plugins displays. There are a couple different ones with the same name in the list, but you want the one by Olivier Lussier. There's nothing wrong with the other ones per se, but if you go to WordPress.org > Extend > Plugins and search for `facebook social plugins`, you see that more people have downloaded this particular one, and that's a rough indicator that you're less likely to have issues.

So find that plugin mentioning Olivier, and then click the Install Now link on the plugin he created. (Thanks, Olivier Lussier.)

After the confirmation message, you can click the Activate Plugin link.

Downloading install package from `http://downloads.wordpress.org/plugin/facebook-social-plugins.1.2.3.zip`...

Unpacking the package...

Installing the plugin...

Successfully installed the plugin **Facebook Social Plugins 1.2.3**.

Activate Plugin | Return to Plugin Installer

This plugin works by creating a few widgets that you can drag into desired positions, just like any other widget.

Next, click Appearance > Widgets.

There will be a few widgets on the left side in the list of available widgets. I suggest trying the FB Activity Feed and FB Like Button.

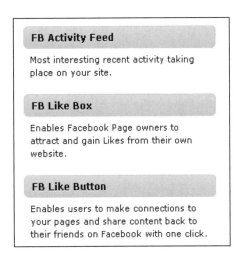

To try out a widget, roll your mouse over it until you get the four-headed mouse pointer, click, and drag up and to the right.

Drop the desired widget into the Primary Widget Area.

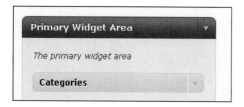

You have a few different options; if you have been following along and are using a similar theme to the one I'm using, you might want to enter in a width of 200 (see Figure 11.1).

Figure 11.1
FB Activity Feed widget.

Then click the Save button and the Close link, and take a look at your blog.

You should theoretically see a panel like this. If you don't see Recent Activity, you might want to make a post on Facebook with a link to your blog and then come back in a few days and see what it says.

CHANGING WIDGET SETTINGS

If you want to go back and change a setting on a widget, click the downward-facing triangle at the right side of one of the widgets (for example, if you don't indicate a width in one of the social plugins and want to change it so that it fits better).

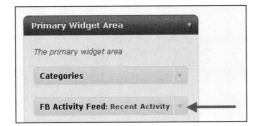

Next, if you like, try dragging over the FB Like Button widget.

Then enter in your setting (for example, indicating a width of 200, or checking Show Faces), click the Save button, and then click the Close link (see Figure 11.2).

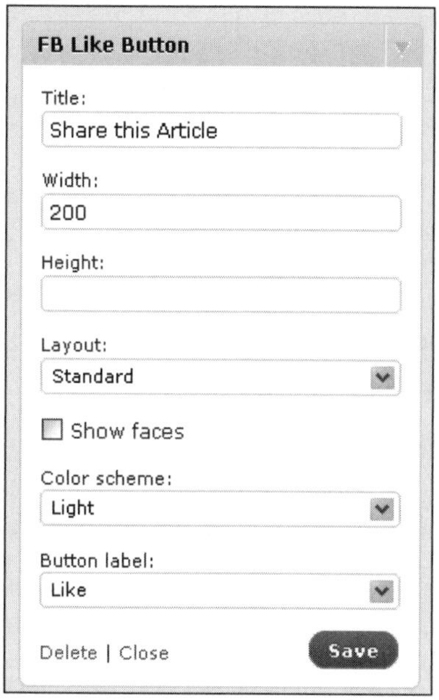

FB Like Button
Title:
Share this Article
Width:
200
Height:
Layout:
Standard
Show faces
Color scheme:
Light
Button label:
Like
Delete | Close
Save

Figure 11.2
FB Like Button widget.

You should see something like this on your blog.

Share this Article
Like
Todd Kelsey likes this.

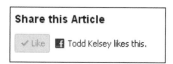

It's not "really" sharing; it's more about a Like button, so you might want to go into the widget and change it to Like This.

The plugin also adds a Like option at the bottom of each article (see Figure 11.3).

To read a bit more about this WordPress plugin, see http://olussier.net/demo/facebook-social-plugins/. To view more info from Facebook on what the plugins are supposed to do, see http://developers.facebook.com/docs/plugins/.

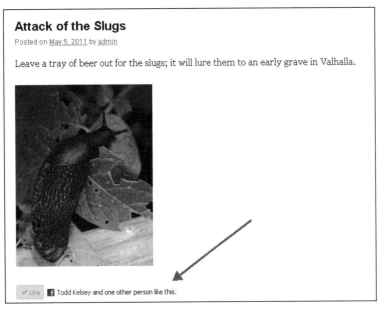

Figure 11.3
The Like button on a post.

GTRANSLATE

Next on our agenda of fun, we'll look at a WordPress plugin that allows you to make your blog available in different languages. Keep in mind that the translation is a computer translation (from Google), so it's not nearly as good as human translation; still, it might help to convey some meaning and can give your blog a international spirit. (Woohoo!)

To get started, visit Plugins in your Dashboard.

Then click the Add New button.

Then type gtranslate in the search box, and click the Search Plugins button.

Next, find GTranslate in the list, and click the Install Now link.

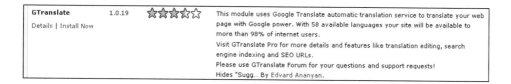

You should get a confirmation message. You can click the Activate Plugin link.

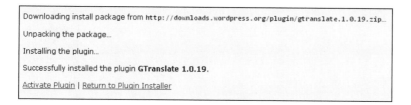

Like the Facebook plugin, this one creates a draggable widget, so go to Appearance > Widgets in the Dashboard.

Then click and drag GTranslate up and to the right, and drop it in the Primary Widgets Area.

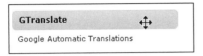

The window has a spot for a title, and a configuration message.

If you like, enter in a title like `Translate`, click Save, and then click the Close link.

Your blog should show something like this.

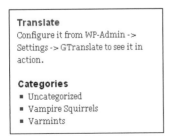

To configure the plugin, visit Settings > GTranslate.

There will be a bunch of options that you can always come back to (see Figure 11.4). For example, you might like to enable additional Flag languages, which you could do by selecting the check boxes. But if you like, you can simply click the Save Changes button without changing anything.

Click the Save Changes button.

Then you should see something like this on your blog. You can click the Select Language drop-down menu and choose another language.

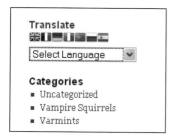

You then see your blog in another language (see Figure 11.5).

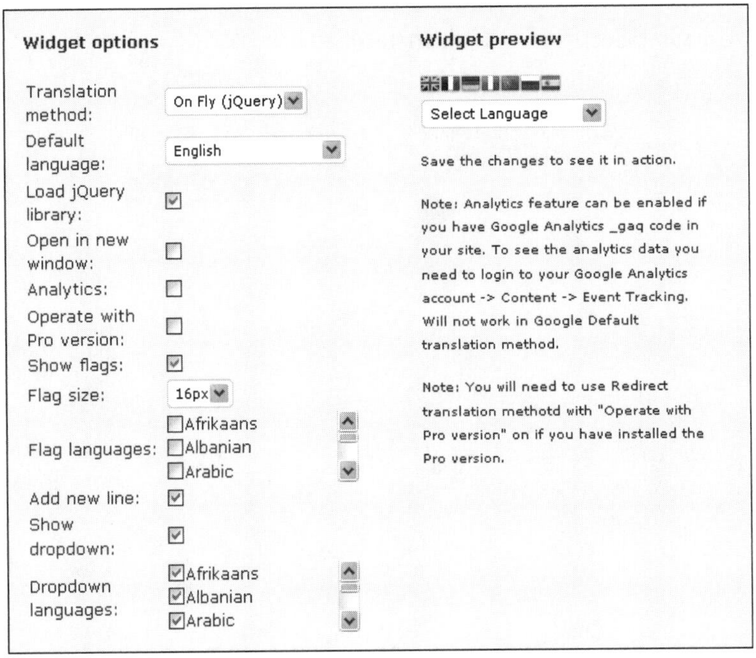

Figure 11.4
GTranslate Widget options.

Figure 11.5
If all the stars align and the plugin works, a translated page results.

If you want to switch back to English and the Translate menu doesn't have English options anymore (gasp!), try clicking on the little British flag.

For more information on GTranslate, including a look at what the Pro version can offer, visit http://edo.webmaster.am/gtranslate?xyz=998 (see Figure 11.6).

GTranslate		
Get translations with a single click between 58 languages (more than 98% of internet users) on your website! Free version is on the list of Top Rated Extensions from JED		
	GTranslate Free	**GTranslate Pro**
Translations between 58 languages + analytics	•	•
Hide Google's top frame after translation	•	•
Language bar with flags	•	•
Hide Google's "Suggest Better Translation" pop-up	•	•
Hide Google's translator IP	•	•
Enable search engine indexing		•
Search engine friendly URLs (/es, /fr, /it, etc.)		•
Cache support with ability to edit translations		•
Meta keywords and meta description translation		•
non-Joomla! websites	Limited	•
Curl library and ionCube loader required		•
Price	Free	€ 59†
Buy using PayPal or Credit Card	Donate	Buy Now

Figure 11.6
GTranslate options.

You might also be interested in making a donation. With all these plugins we've been looking at, the people who create them are basically volunteer programmers, so if you have an extra dollar or more, I'm sure they would appreciate your support. To find the developer for a particular plugin, go to http://wordpress.org/extend/plugins/, look for the plugin page, and look for a Donate link.

SHARE ON FACEBOOK

Another thing you might like to do, to increase the chances of people sharing your articles with their friends on Facebook, is install a Share plugin of some kind. If you go to Plugins > Add New > Search as we have with other plugins, and type in `share on facebook`, a few different options come up. There's one called Add This that is popular. It adds a lot of icons for just about every social network, including Twitter.

For this example, we'll look at one simply called Share on Facebook. I recommend starting there and then looking at some of the others if you would like people to be able to share on Twitter and other sites.

To find our example plugin, as per usual, go to Plugins in the Dashboard, click the Add New button/link, and in the search box, enter `share on facebook`. Having found it, click Install Now.

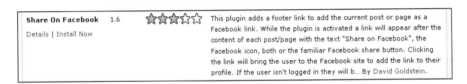

Then activate it as usual, and you get a Share on Facebook link at the bottom of your posts.

The link opens a standard Share window. If you're not logged into Facebook, you're asked to log in first, and then you can include a comment and click the Share Link button.

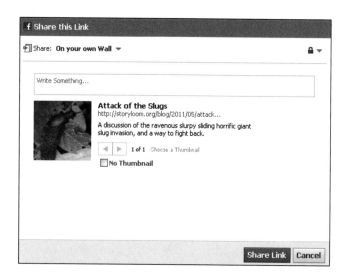

You wind up with something like this on your Facebook wall (which also appears in your friends' news feeds).

Sweet.

Conclusion

Dear Reader,

Woohoo! We took a look in this chapter at a couple ways to connect with the wider world. I recommend getting familiar with the Facebook social plugin, because it can help create more connections between your blog and the world of Facebook, where people are spending increasing amounts of time.

When people click on the Like button on your blog, theoretically a little message appears in all their friends' news feeds, which can help you get exposure. So you might like to try some things on your blog and then invite people not only to visit it, but to click on the Like button. Or, for example, you might include an invitation on your Welcome or About page on your blog to click the Like button.

All this social tie-in stuff is important because the easier you make it for people to share, or like, or cross-pollenate with other social networks, the more traffic your blog gets. Show and tell!

I invite you to consider adding the GTranslate plugin. If you get that international feeling, explore the GTranslate Pro option and see if you can get a human translator to help you make a bona fide Spanish translation of a blog article, for example.

Then, of course, if you get as excited about multilingual sites as I do, drop me an email at tekelsey@gmail.com and I'll send you a copy of my dissertation, which discusses using open source content management systems to develop multilingual sites. (WordPress is an open source content management system. See http://en.wikipedia.org/wiki/WordPress if you haven't already.) If enough people ask for it, I'll post it on www.wordpressprimer.net.

May the world get ever smaller, and may all the colors bleed into one, as Bono once sang.

Regards,

Todd

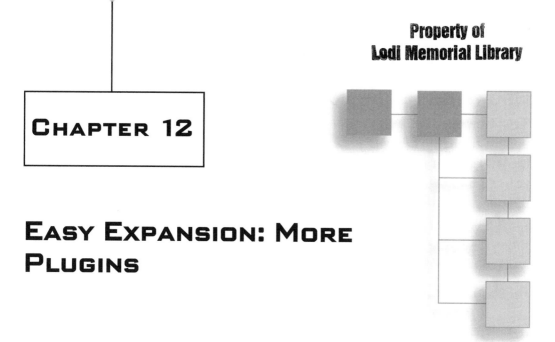

CHAPTER 12

EASY EXPANSION: MORE PLUGINS

In This Chapter:

- Browsing Plugins
- Subscribing to an Email List
- Exploring the Yet Another Related Posts Plugin
- Adding Videos to Your Blog Posts
- Activating WP-reCAPTCHA
- Perusing WP e-Commerce

The purpose of this chapter is to look at a selection of additional plugins that you might find helpful for using with your WordPress site. I recommend considering a Subscribe function to make it easier for people to hear about new posts on your blog. The Related Posts feature is an extra, but it's probably worth exploring as a technique, if not for the plugin itself. Similarly, there's a nice YouTube plugin that can help you include YouTube videos.

WP-reCAPTCHA is the one plugin I would recommend adding for this chapter if you had to choose only one, because it helps to reduce spam.

For those interested in the idea of selling merchandise at some point through a blog, we take a look at WP e-Commerce.

BROWSING PLUGINS

At some point, you might want to visit the WordPress.org site and browse for plugins using the following link, which highlights the most popular ones. There are *a lot* of WordPress plugins, and you needn't keep to only the most popular if you are looking for something specific. But in general, the more popular the plugin, the higher the chance that there is one or more developers (volunteer developers) keeping the plugin going and making sure it is up to date. And as a rule, if you can afford it, I suggest donating something to the projects—perhaps $1 or more for each plugin you use.

http://wordpress.org/extend/plugins/browse/popular/

Figure 12.1 shows the first page of results for the most popular plugins at the time of writing. Some of them have been covered already in the book.

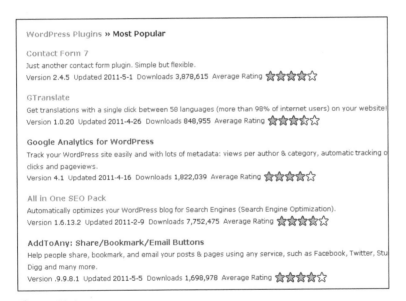

Figure 12.1
The most popular plugins at the time of writing.

To look through more, click the Next button at the bottom.

SUBSCRIBING TO AN EMAIL LIST

Subscribing to an email list can be tricky. In the free version of WordPress, there is an email subscription widget that you can drag over into your Primary widget area, but the disadvantage is that it requires someone to already have a WordPress account or to create one. Other techniques involve a tool called FeedBurner, but it can also be tricky to install/configure.

The Subscribe2 plugin is pretty popular, offers flexibility, and keeps things simple. It might work right out of the box, or not, but I think it is worth trying. Initially, when I tried the Subscribe link, the plugin treated me as a user of the blog as opposed to a random visitor, but then a few minutes later it seemed to catch up and worked okay. So it is worth trying. Welcome to the wild west of open source software.

To get the Subscribe2 plugin, go to Dashboard > Plugins > Add New Plugin, enter `subscribe2` in the search box, and click Search Plugins.

Then click Install Now.

After installation, click Activate Plugin.

If you like, scroll down to the entry in the list of plugins and explore the Donate link, or click the Settings link.

On the Settings screen (also available in the Dashboard under Settings > Subscribe2), try clicking the Send Email Preview button.

You should receive an email that is something like this.

Depending on your email settings, Subscribe2 should open and show the post (see Figure 12.2).

Figure 12.2
Email with blog post preview.

To access the Settings page, go to Settings > Subscribe2 in the Dashboard (see Figure 12.3).

Figure 12.3
The contents of the Setting area depend on what plugins you've installed.

There's a host of settings you can tweak. We'll take a look at some high-level options. For starters, on the Settings page, click Enable Subscribe2 Widget; this enables a widget that can be positioned on the page to allow people to subscribe.

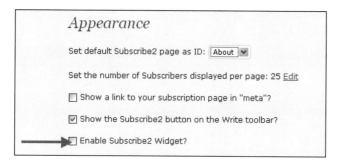

And be sure to click the Submit button on the Settings page.

Then in the Dashboard, go to Appearance > Widgets.

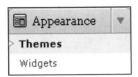

And drag the Subscribe2 widget into the Primary Widget area.

The widget pops open in the standard way (see Figure 12.4).

Figure 12.4
Subcribe2 widget.

I suggest changing the title to something like Subscribe To This Blog to make things clear.

Then click the Save button and the Close link.

If you look at your blog, you will probably see something like this.

If you get a You may manage your subscription options message, you may be an official, logged-in user of the blog. To see what others will see, open a different browser (for example, if you are using Internet Explorer, open Firefox, Chrome, or Safari) and visit your blog. You should see a more standard Subscribe panel.

You might like to have a friend try subscribing or try subscribing yourself to test the options.

EXPLORING THE YET ANOTHER RELATED POSTS PLUGIN

Having related posts can be a helpful way of getting a person to read more on your blog. A friend of mine who is a Chinese blogger has consistently added links at the end of their blog posts to other blog posts they've made, along with a message like If you liked this post, you might also be interested in:. And as their blog has grown, so has the amount of "repeat traffic" coming from those related links. So you could certainly get in that habit, but there are some other solutions out there.

The Yet Another Related Posts plugin attempts to do some automatic calculation. If you don't mind tweaking things a bit, you might be able to get some action out of it. This plugin probably works better with longer posts and when you use tags in your posts. (We'll take a look at how to add a tag.)

To get the plugin, go to Dashboard > Plugins > Add New Plugin.

Enter `yet another related` in the search box, and click the Search Plugins button.

Click on the Install Now link.

And click on the Activate Plugin link.

If you scroll down in the list of plugins, you might like to visit the plugin site.

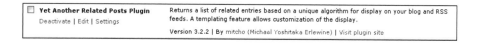

Otherwise, go to Appearance > Widgets, and click and drag the widget into the Primary Widget area.

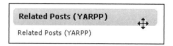

If you don't want `YARPP` to appear in the panel, enter a new title, such as `Related Posts`. When you're done, click the Save button and the Close link.

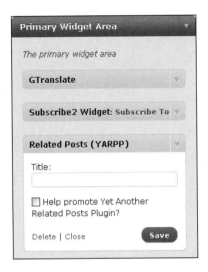

The panel might display like this on your blog, depending on how many posts you have and how YARPP crunches through your posts. It attempts to do this automatically. Once it is installed, if it doesn't seem to be picking things up, you might want to deactivate it. (Go to Plugins, find the plugin in the list, and click Deactivate.) Then come back and activate it later on to see if it picks up anything, based on clicking on some individual posts.

To access the Settings page, click Settings > Related Posts (YARPP).

The settings screen has a number of options you can try tweaking if the automated default settings don't seem to be working.

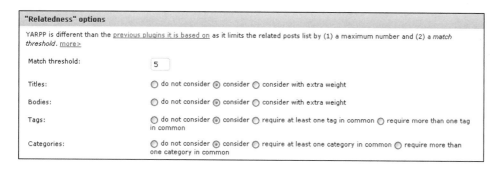

One thing that will probably help is to add tags to posts, which provides more information for YARPP to crunch.

To add tags, go to Posts; either add a new post, or find one of your existing ones in the list and click on its title to edit it.

When you're creating a post or editing an existing one, look for the Post Tags panel.

Enter a tag (similar to a category—a descriptive term that you might enter on multiple related posts), such as gardening, and click the Add button.

The tag will appear.

Be sure to then click the Update button (or Publish, if it is a new post).

Then go through and try adding tags to a few posts to see what happens.

If you just go to the main address of your blog (for example, www.storyloom. org/blog), nothing might show up because there isn't an individual post selected.

You might need to click on the title of a post.

Otherwise, if the plugin doesn't work for you, you can always deactivate it. Also, keep in mind that if you categorize posts and have a nice list of categories on your blog, you might not need tags. Categories are kind of an equivalent—people who are interested in particular themes might naturally see your list of categories or table of contents and click to explore more. Another way to help promote posts without bothering with tags is to have links at the end of your posts; and if you don't want to go to the trouble of adding links at the end of your blog posts to other articles, you can always just say this: If you like this post, check out the_____ category in the upper-right corner of the blog, to see more posts on_____ .

ADDING VIDEOS TO YOUR BLOG POSTS

In this section, we take a look at two techniques for adding videos to your blog posts.

Using Smart YouTube to Add Videos

I encourage you to consider including YouTube videos when possible in blog posts to keep things interesting. If you are talking about a particular theme and want to add more material, search YouTube, and chances are there are videos on the topic. You can then embed the videos in your posts.

What the Smart YouTube plugin does is allow you to simply paste a YouTube video link in your post, like this.

http://www.youtube.com/watch?v=0jkOeJ5T3Lg

Then YouTube automatically embeds the video, so that instead of just having the link to the video, a person can watch it right in your blog post.

To get the plugin, go to Dashboard > Plugins > Add New Plugin.

Search for Smart YouTube in the search box on that screen, and click the Install Now link.

Name	Version	Rating	Description
Smart YouTube Details | Install Now	3.8.6	☆☆☆☆☆	Smart Youtube is a Wordpress Youtube Plugin that allows you to easily insert Youtube videos/playlists in your post, comments and in RSS feed. The main purpose of the plugin is to correctly embed youtube videos into your blog post. The video will be shown in full in your RSS feed as well. Smart youtube also supports playback of high quality videos, works on iPhone, produces xHTML valid code (unli... By Vladimir Prelovac.

Then click the Activate Plugin link.

To get a YouTube video link, go to www.youtube.com and click on any video you like. For example, type a topic or theme in the search box at the top, and click the Search button.

Then select a video.

The link that appears in the top of your browser window is what you want.

To copy it, you can click to select it, and then right-click (Windows)/Ctrl-click (Mac) and choose Copy.

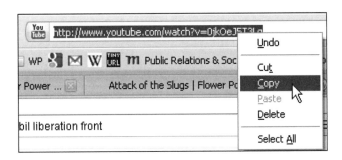

Then paste the link into a post.

Gerbil Liberation Front

Permalink: http://storyloom.org/blog/2011/05/gerbil-liberation-front/ (Edit)

Upload/Insert 🖼 🎞 ♫ ⚙   Visual HTML

B *I* ABC ⚏ ⚏ ⚏ 66 ☰ ☰ ☰ 🔗 ✂ 🗔 ▼ 🖥 ⚏ S2

Here is a video called "Chew"

http://www.youtube.com/watch?v=ojkOeJ5T3Lg

Click Publish (new post) or Update (existing post).

Theoretically, you should see something like this (see Figure 12.5). For me, the video appeared at a larger size than I wanted. That's why we also talk about the

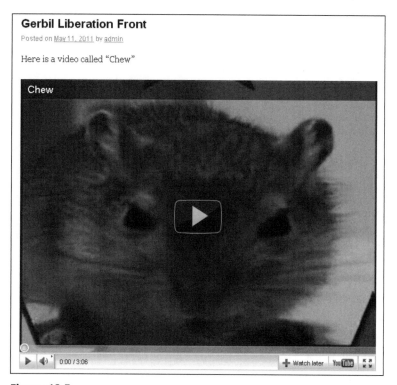

Figure 12.5
A video within a post.

traditional method of embedding a video in the next section, which involves copying a bit of code from YouTube. You might not have the same issue I did; welcome to open source.

If you like, you can try to tweak settings by going to Settings > Smart Youtube.

Then you can click the leftmost box in the Normal Mode area.

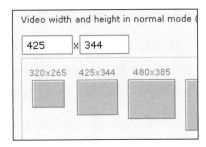

Also click the leftmost box in the High Quality area.

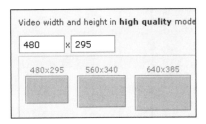

And then you can click Update Options.

Embedding a Video Manually

Here is the traditional way to embed a video, which takes a bit more effort but might be more reliable.

First, find your video on YouTube.

Then, on the YouTube page, scroll down and click the Share button. You get a pop-up area; click the Embed button.

Then select the code in the little box (`<iframe>`*blah*`</iframe>`, and so on) and copy it into memory (Ctrl+C).

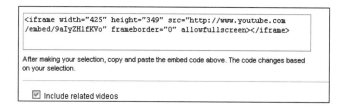

Next, go into a post in WordPress, and click on the HTML tab.

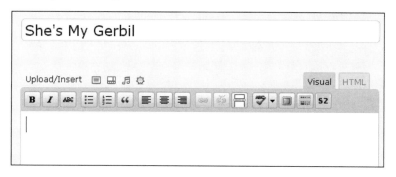

Paste in the code.

Then be sure to click the Publish button.

If you like, when you do this, you can click the Visual tab, and enter text to accompany the YouTube video.

Then you should see something like this on the blog.

ACTIVATING WP-reCAPTCHA

This plugin is worth installing and activating simply because it reduces the amount of comment spam you get.

To obtain the plugin, go to Dashboard > Plugins > Add New Plugin.

Search for wp recaptcha, and click the Search Plugins button.

Then click the Install Now button.

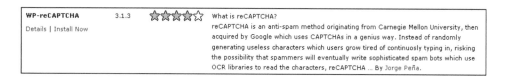

And click the Activate Plugin link.

You get a message that mentions API (application programming interface) keys. You need to get a code to activate the plugin, but it is worth it, because doing so takes less time relative to the spam you would otherwise get. It's not perfect, but it helps.

Click the Fix This link.

To get going, click on the Here link in the `you can get the keys here` message on the Settings page for the plugin.

I recommend right-clicking (Windows) or Ctrl-clicking (Mac) and opening the link in a new tab. That way you don't lose your Dashboard screen.

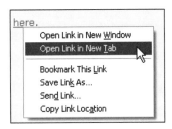

To get the API key, you need to sign in with a Google/Gmail account. If you're already signed into Gmail, you won't see this screen. If you don't have an account, I highly recommend creating a Gmail account; just visit http://mail.google.com.

After logging in, theoretically your domain will automatically appear, as shown in Figure 12.6 (for example, storyloom.org in the graphic that follows). A domain is another name for a website address ending in .com, .net, .org, and so on. If the address doesn't appear, just type it in. Even if your blog is at a subaddress, just use the main one. A subaddress would be something like http://storyloom.org/blog, but what they're looking for here is the main address.

But if the address is filled in correctly for you and it's right, just click Create Key.

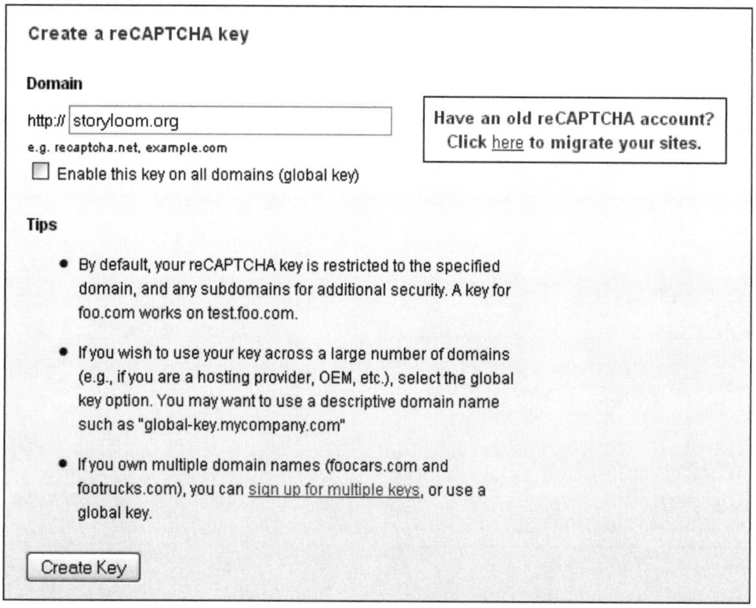

Figure 12.6
Creating a WP-reCAPTCHA key to bring back into WordPress. The Web address you use for your blog theoretically appears in the box at the top; if it doesn't, fill in the correct address.

Then copy the public key and private key into the WordPress settings screen (see Figure 12.7).

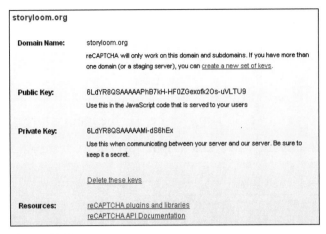

Figure 12.7
The public and private key that you use with WP-reCAPTCHA.

Paste the keys in the correct spots.

And click the Save reCAPTCHA Changes button.

Then visit your blog, perhaps in another browser, and at the bottom of a post, click Leave a Comment.

You should see something like this. What WP-reCAPTCHA is doing is making it harder for automated spammers to add comment spam to your blog.

It's not perfect; some folks have hired humans to sit there and type in these codes and interface them with spam programs. But you do what you can in the spam wars.

Perusing WP e-Commerce

Last but not least, we take a wee peek at a plugin that can help you set up a store on your WordPress blog.

If you decide to try out this plugin, be aware that it can create pages that you'll have to delete; it also seems to interfere with a plugin called RSS Graffiti mentioned in Chapter 13, "Promoting on Social Media." When I came back and deactivated WP e-Commerce, I had to go into Dashboard > Pages and delete several pages that WP e-Commerce had created. If you can see WP e-Commerce as an experiment and don't mind the possibility of creating a mess that you need to clean up, you might be interested in using your hosting account to create a test blog at an address like www.yourwebsite.com/test and try plugins there before you add them to your main blog.

To get the WP e-Commerce plugin, go to Dashboard > Plugins > Add New Plugin.

Then type in WP e-Commerce, capitalized upper-/lowercase exactly as it appears in this sentence, and click the Search Plugins button.

Then click the Install Now link.

Alternatively, just visit http://getshopped.org/ to get background info (see Figure 12.8).

Figure 12.8
WP e-Commerce options.

And, if you like, remember that you can always go to Plugins, find WP e-Commerce, and click Deactivate. There's also a link here for the www. getshopped.org site, the support forum, and the documentation.

Basically what the plugin does is add a page on your blog, which you can use to sell stuff.

If you want to try tweaking a few things without reading the documentation or visiting the site, you can dive in by clicking Dashboard > Store Sales. There will be some information there, but I highly recommend visiting www.getshopped. org and wandering around if you're interested in trying out WP e-Commerce.

If you've had enough of a taste, go to Plugins, and deactivate WP e-Commerce. You can always reactivate it sometime in the future.

CONCLUSION

Dear Reader,

Congratulations on making it through this whirlwind tour of some additional plugins! I think each is worth looking at. At this point, I encourage you to try exploring plugins and adding some yourself.

There's a bit of a catch-22. Theoretically, you should be able to add plugins without them conflicting with each other. If you see Update links in your Dashboard, you should act on them. (Sometimes new releases of plugins correct bugs or help a new version of a plugin interact with a new version of WordPress.) But if you end up adding a plugin and notice other plugins acting weird, you can always deactivate them.

Also, the principle of trying plugins that are popular reduces the chances of your having an issue.

You might just want to keep things simple. As for this chapter, if you want to keep things as simple as possible, I would at least investigate WP-reCAPTCHA.

Another approach is to use your hosting account to make a test blog at another address so you can try plugins like WP e-Commerce in a controlled environment. That way, you reduce the chance of conflicts with other plugins and apps.

Best wishes!

Regards,

Todd

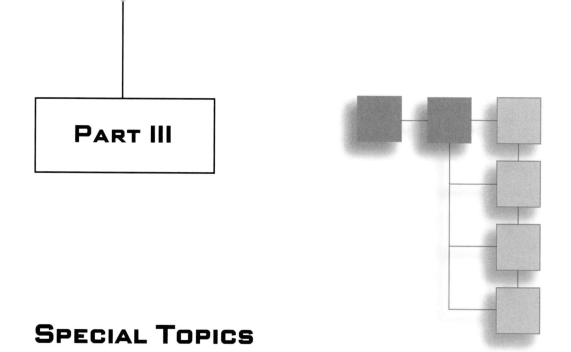

PART III

SPECIAL TOPICS

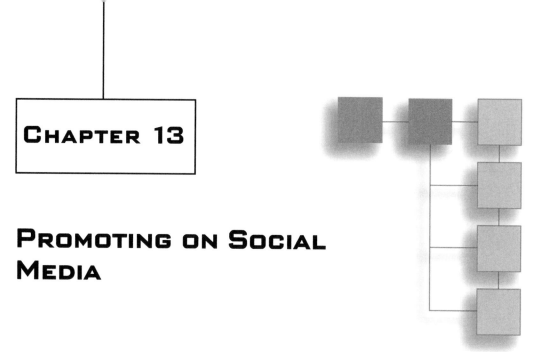

CHAPTER 13

PROMOTING ON SOCIAL MEDIA

In This Chapter:

- Copying a Link into Facebook
- Importing a Blog into Your Personal Profile
- Promoting Your Blog on a Facebook Page
- Connecting a Blog to a Facebook Page

The purpose of this chapter is to scratch the surface of social promotion for your WordPress blog. There are a lot of options, but the general idea is to get acquainted with social networks and then find ways to share your blog posts on them. This could be as simple as pasting a link on your own personal Facebook account whenever you make a post on your blog or trying one of the import functions so that whenever you make a post on your blog, it is imported automatically into Facebook.

Another thing you might like to consider is making a Facebook page related to your blog. When you have a Facebook page, it allows you to share your blog posts with anyone who visits the page or clicks the Like button on it.

Don't worry if you're not on Facebook. You can join! (If you're not sure where to start, try downloading the free sample edition of the book *Social Networking Spaces*, from http://tinyurl.com/snspacessed.)

COPYING A LINK INTO FACEBOOK

This is the easiest, simplest method of social promotion; just get in the habit of copying the link for your blog post into Facebook and clicking the Share button.

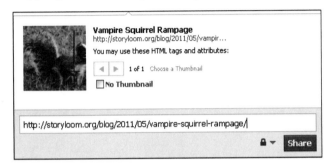

For some reason, the preview function may include a statement like You may use these HTML tags and attributes. Until WordPress corrects that issue, you might have to live with it. I tried looking at a number of different obscure WordPress plugins to correct the issue, and none of them seemed to work.

IMPORTING A BLOG INTO YOUR PERSONAL PROFILE

The next step up from copying and pasting a link for each post into Facebook is to set it up so that blog posts are imported automatically.

At the time of writing, this function was having issues, so if it doesn't work, you can always copy and paste a link or try using the RSS Graffiti Facebook application, described in the next section.

To get started, visit www.facebook.com/editnotes.php.

Then enter the address of your blog feed by adding /feed/ to the end of your blog (for example, http://storyloom.org/blog/feed/).

Then click the check box at the bottom and click the Start Importing button.

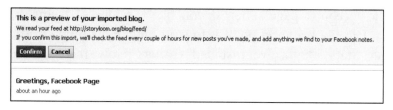

If you get this far, it's a good sign. I had repeated issues when I clicked on the Confirm button on the next page.

If you have issues, I recommend promoting your blog on a Facebook page, connecting a blog to a Facebook page, and installing RSS Graffiti.

PROMOTING YOUR BLOG ON A FACEBOOK PAGE

One reason you might like to consider creating a Facebook page is that it makes it easier for people to see posts about your blog, especially if they are not your friends on Facebook.

Not only can you copy links and post them on your Facebook page in the same way that you might do on your personal profile, you can *advertise* your Facebook page. People are spending so much time on social networks such as Facebook that anything you can do to make it easier for them to get to your blog, the better.

Will people bother to manually come and check your blog? Perhaps. Will people subscribe to your blog by email if you add that function? Possibly.

What if you make it as easy as possible for a person to view your content? Probably the easiest way for people to view your blog posts (if they're spending a fair amount of time on Facebook each week) is to Like a Facebook page. When people Like the Facebook page, any post that appears on the Facebook page appears in their News Feed. In other words, whenever you copy a link to your blog, it appears for them. Nice and easy.

So Facebook pages make sense. In the next chapter, we look at how you can make a Facebook advertisement for your blog. You might like to try advertising the address of your blog directly, or you might like to try advertising your actual Facebook page (it might be easier for someone on Facebook just to click the Like button and get your posts automatically) rather than going to your blog, where it takes more effort to subscribe, and so on.

The best strategy is debatable, but if you like the idea of promotion, I'd suggest at least trying to make a Facebook page. Then if you like the idea of trying an advertisement, create a Facebook ad and point it to your blog. How much traffic do you get with that Stats plugin we installed earlier? How many email subscriptions do you get with the Subscribe2 plugin we installed earlier? Then try running a Facebook advertising campaign separately, which promotes your Facebook page, and see how many Likes you get.

Getting people to subscribe to your blog by email is more effective because they get an email whenever you post something. In contrast, when people Like a Facebook page, they get new posts in their news feed when they log in, but they might miss them.

So my recommendation is to try a few different strategies and see how they work for you.

To explore Facebook pages, visit www.facebook.com/pages.

To create one, just click the Create Page button.

+ Create Page

Figure 13.1 shows a sample Facebook page (http://facebook.com/rgbgreen).

Figure 13.1
Sample Facebook page.

To learn more about Facebook pages, visit http://tinyurl.com/fbpageshelp. There's some basic information on Facebook pages in the Facebook Help section.

CONNECTING A BLOG TO A FACEBOOK PAGE

When you make a Facebook page, you can paste links on it using the old-fashioned method, but you also have options for importing blogs automatically. We'll look at one called RSS Graffiti, which is fairly popular.

For our example, we'll use the *Getting Started with WordPress* Facebook page.

At the moment, it has a long address:

> www.facebook.com/pages/Getting-Started-with-WordPress/
> 186134644744074

When you create a Facebook page, you get a long address, but as soon as you have 25 Likes, you can go to http://facebook.com/username and choose a shorter address. For example, when I started the RGBGreen Facebook page, I made a Facebook advertising campaign, and as soon as I had 25 likes, I requested "RGBGreen" as a Facebook page username, and it resulted in www.facebook.com/RGBgreen.

To get started with the process of connecting a blog, go to your Facebook page, and click the Edit Page link (see Figure 13.2). (Notice how Facebook shows you

Figure 13.2
Editing a page when logged in.

what an ad "could" look like, in the lower-right corner of your Facebook page. More on that in the next chapter.)

What we'll be doing is adding a plugin that imports blog posts into a feature of Facebook called Notes (which are like blog posts in many ways). On your personal profile in Facebook, the Notes feature is typically enabled from the get-go. With a Facebook page, you might need to enable it.

After clicking Edit Page, select the Apps icon on the left.

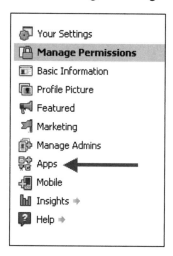

In the list of apps, find Notes, and click the Edit Settings link.

Click the Add link.

Then click the Okay button.

Next, click the View Page button to look at the page.

On your Facebook page, you should now see the Notes icon on the left.

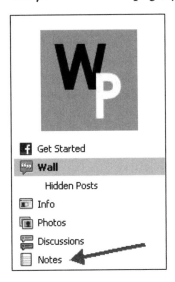

To try out the Notes feature, click the Write a Note button or link.

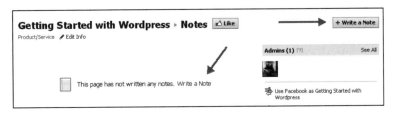

The Notes feature works pretty much like a blog post. Enter some text, and click the Publish button (see Figure 13.3).

Figure 13.3
Writing a Note.

You get a confirmation message. Then you can click the link directly beneath the title of your Note (for example, Hello world) to get back to your page. In this case, the link is Getting Started with WordPress.

Then you see how making a Note resulted in a post on your Facebook page (see Figure 13.4). When you connect your blog and automatically import posts via the Notes feature, this is the way they appear.

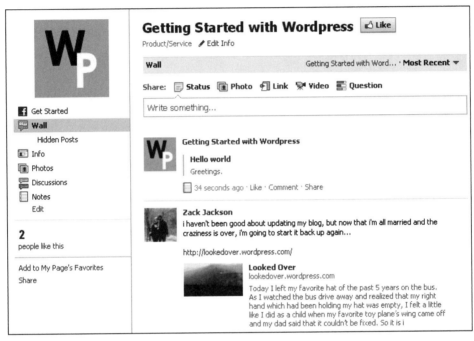

Figure 13.4
Creating a Note results in a post on your Facebook page.

Installing RSS Graffiti

RSS Graffiti is a popular Facebook application that allows you to connect your blog to your Facebook account and do other similar things. A Facebook application is simply software that you can load into your Facebook account to add new features or to play games.

To get started, visit www.facebook.com/RSS.Graffiti and click the Go to App button (see Figure 13.5).

You can also go directly to http://apps.facebook.com/rssgraffiti/.

Figure 13.5
RSS Graffiti home page on Facebook.

On the App page, look at the information shown in Figure 13.6.

In particular, check out the Setup Checklist. Basically, it's saying that you need to authorize the application to do some things on your behalf—namely get your blog posts and then use your Facebook account to add them to the desired spot, such as a Facebook page.

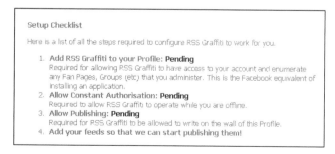

Figure 13.6
When you add the application, you need to configure various settings.

To begin, click the Click Here to Authorize RSS Graffiti button.

Then click the Allow button (see Figure 13.7). Nothing on the Internet is 100% secure, but authorizing this app is a reasonable risk, in part because a million people are using it.

Figure 13.7
Authorizing Facebook.

After you authorize the app, the screen should look something like this.

On the lower-left side is a list of any Facebook pages you've created (see Figure 13.8).

Figure 13.8
The authorized app can now be used for its purpose.

Then click on the link for the Facebook page you want to connect your blog to.

You'll see a screen like this. Select the Click Here to Add RSS Graffiti to This Fan Page button (see Figure 13.9).

Then click the Add RSS Graffiti button.

Figure 13.9
Once the application is ready, you can add it to specific Facebook pages.

Next, click the Click to Authorize button if you see a message like this.

Then click the Allow button.

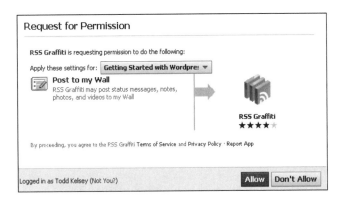

Finally, you should see a screen like this, where you can click the Add Feed button.

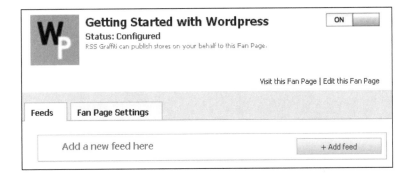

What we will be doing is adding a feed. A *feed* is a way of enabling a person (or a program) to subscribe to a blog. Many people read blogs using programs like Google Reader, and what reader programs do is connect to a feed. The feed announces when a new post has been made. In this case, RSS Graffiti is taking the blog posts from the feed and posting them on Facebook automatically.

In the screen that pops up, enter the address of your blog feed in the Feed URL box.

To get the feed address, take your blog address.

For example: http://storyloom.org/blog

and add /feed/

For example: http://storyloom.org/blog/feed/

After pasting the link, click the Click Here to Fetch and Preview It link (see the previous image).

You should get a preview of your blog. Then you can click the Save button.

Remember, if you have issues such as the preview not appearing and reporting "empty feed," and if you tried installing the WP e-Commerce plugin from the previous chapter, you might need to deactivate that plugin before being able to use RSS Graffiti.

Next, try making a post on your blog.

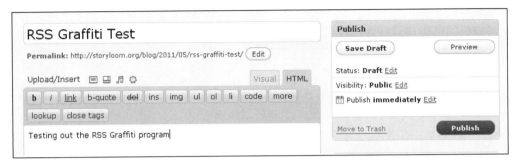

Then cross your fingers and check back on your Facebook page in a bit. Ideally, your post will appear there. If it doesn't appear in 10–15 minutes, make a new post. If that one doesn't appear the next day, I recommend going back to the manual method of copying and pasting blog post links on your Facebook page. Welcome to the world of open source content management system meets Facebook meets third-party Facebook application. Things don't always work, so it's good to have a backup plan.

Accessing RSS Graffiti

After you have the RSS Graffiti Facebook app installed, you should be able to click the Home link in Facebook to access it.

It should appear on the left side of the screen.

Importing Your Blog Posts into Your Personal Profile

If you get RSS Graffiti working and want to try importing your blog into your personal profile (especially if the link I provided earlier in the chapter doesn't work), look for the Your Profile section in RSS Graffiti.

By clicking on your name (for example, Todd Kelsey), you can add a feed the same way you did with a Facebook page. Theoretically, you can import your blog posts into your personal account for more automatic exposure. Best wishes!

Going Mobile

If you really get into the social promotion stuff, you might also be interested in going mobile. Increasing numbers of people are spending time on their mobile devices, and there's a plugin called WP Touch that can help make a "mobile friendly" version of your blog.

To check out the plugin, visit http://wordpress.org/extend/plugins/wptouch/.

If you would like to install it, go to your Dashboard > Plugins > Add New. Then search for WP Touch.

CONCLUSION

Dear Reader,

Whoowhee! In this chapter, we looked at how to share things on Facebook. Even if all you did was paste blog post links to your personal profile on a regular basis, that would be considered social media marketing. But a Facebook page is worth considering, and yes, in spite of the hoops you have to jump through with no guarantee of success, RSS Graffiti and automatic import are also worth looking into. If you can get those working, they make things automatic and offer flexibility.

Best wishes!

Regards,

Todd

CHAPTER 14

PROMOTING WITH SOCIAL ADVERTISING

In This Chapter:

- Getting Over Intimidation
- Creating a Facebook Ad
- Accessing Ads
- Making an Ad for a Facebook Page
- Reviewing Performance
- Starting a Revolution (or Helping One)
- Learning More About Facebook Advertising
- Investigating Other Kinds of Social Advertising

The purpose of this chapter is to introduce you to the concept of social advertising—that is, using something like Facebook ads to promote your blog or a Facebook page. The least expensive form of promotion is to go out on social networks and make posts, develop relationships in online communities with people of similar interests and share your blog with them, search for influential blogs, and start commenting on posts and seeing if the authors will make a post about your blog (or at least include a link to your blog in comments). All of these "grassroots" forms of promotion are worth trying, but sometimes spending money makes sense—especially if you have a product to sell or an organization to promote, or if you just want to get a bit of initial momentum.

The same question comes up here—to Facebook or not to Facebook? There's nothing wrong with having no Facebook presence for a blog, but if you're interested in the discussion from the previous chapter about the idea of making a Facebook page as an extension of your blog and making it as easy as possible for people to subscribe, Like, and otherwise connect, a social presence *does* make sense.

In the context of social advertising, you can run a direct ad to your blog. We'll look at that first. You could invite people to come and look at your blog, and if you have any of the social plugins implemented that we discussed in earlier chapters, people could click the Like button directly on your blog or share your blog articles with their friends. You might find that people do this even if you have no Facebook presence. You could tell this if you installed Google Analytics (prior chapter) and looked at where people are coming from or installed the Stats plugin. If you start seeing traffic coming from Facebook, people are posting your blog on Facebook somewhere.

I suggest trying both, actually—starting out perhaps by trying a direct Facebook ad and seeing if it results in some traffic to your blog. (Remember to add some doodads to your blog, such as an email subscription, a Like button, or a Share on Facebook link—and remember to have some blog posts on there.) Also try to make a Facebook page, and advertise it. Compare the two: how much traffic did you get to your blog as a result of the direct ad campaign? How many email subscriptions surfaced? How much traffic did you get to your Facebook page? How many Likes did you get? And when you're doing this, it might help to run one campaign and then the other (not at the same time) so that you can compare the performance of the two.

You might also try including a sentence at the end of each blog post, such as, "Like this article? Please share on Facebook." Sometimes it helps to make an overt invitation.

GETTING OVER INTIMIDATION

I used to feel intimidated by online advertising. It seemed too complex and overwhelming and had too many details. Mainly this was in relation to Google Advertising and the mysterious world of search engine optimization. There were people where I worked whose full-time job was to do these things, and they seemed like wizards to me.

Then one time I tried making an ad on Facebook, and it was pretty easy. I was surprised.

It was also fun!

So I encourage you to try making a Facebook ad and see how it goes. Don't be surprised if it leads you to develop an interest in online marketing as a hobby, as a career, or even as a volunteer (to help a nonprofit organization). Go for it!

CREATING A FACEBOOK AD

To create a Facebook ad, start a Facebook account at www.facebook.com (or use your existing one).

Then visit www.facebook.com/advertising/ and click the Create an Ad button (see Figure 14.1).

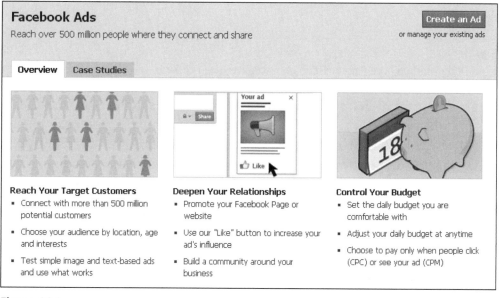

Figure 14.1
Facebook Ads welcome page.

Take a look at the Design Your Ad screen, shown in Figure 14.2. Then start clicking! In this graphic, I point out all the little links and question marks, which have information about what the various options are and what they involve. I suggest clicking on every one, because doing so helps you develop the habit of exploring for information.

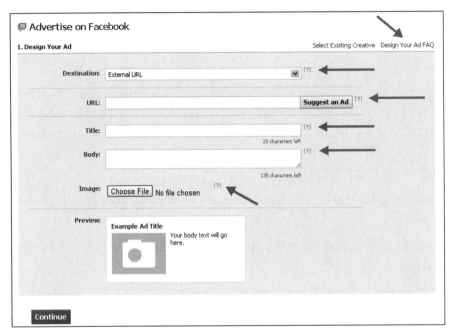

Figure 14.2
The Ad Design section, including question marks that you can click on.

On this screen, the default setting is External URL, which simply means that the ad points to whatever you want it to (such as your blog, at http://storyloom.org/blog). But while we're here, we'll look at what you can do if you do have a Facebook page. The Destination drop-down menu also allows you to select a Facebook page, if you would like to point an ad there. Selecting a Facebook page involves some different options, including Sponsored Stories. We'll come back to this later.

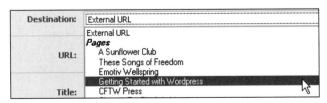

For the moment, set the Destination drop-down menu to External URL, and then enter the address of your blog into the URL field.

Then enter a title (there's a limit on characters) and some text for the ad. I wouldn't worry too much about what specific text you use at this point; just try to keep it brief, as if you only had a moment to speak to someone, and you were inviting him to visit your blog. You could make a proactive statement, like "Come and see!", or it could be just a description. Try a few things (using a separate document, if you like), and imagine if you were looking at the ad. Would it be compelling to you?

As you try different titles and body text, a little preview of the ad appears at the bottom (see Figure 14.3).

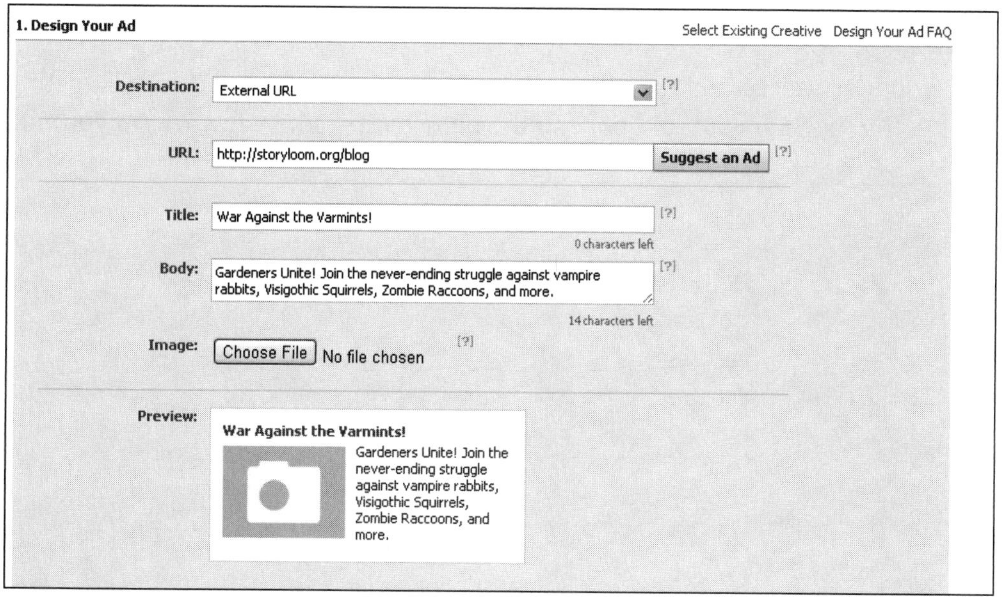

Figure 14.3
Sample information, and a preview of the ad.

Next, you'll want to add a picture. Try something interesting, unusual, or compelling. What would get your attention? The picture could be just about anything. Take a picture yourself, learn how to scan something, or find a picture at www.publicdomainpictures.net or www.istockphoto.com.

When you have a picture you would like to use, click the Choose File button, locate your picture on the computer, and double-click on it. It uploads and is added to the preview.

Then click the Continue button.

Continue

Next, you'll try targeting specific people, as shown in Figure 14.4. Targeting allows you to narrow your audience to the people most likely to click on your ad.

Figure 14.4
Targeting allows you to focus on particular groups of people.

The targeting could involve a certain region, age, gender, or just about any interest/activity you can think of.

On the right side of the screen, Facebook keeps a running total of how many people fit that description. It doesn't mean this is how many people are going to see the ad, and it doesn't mean this is how many people will click it, but it gives you a general idea.

Without changing anything, at the time of writing, there are about 140 million people living in the United States who are 18 or older who would see the ad as I'm trying it now.

To try targeting, you might like to enter one or more interests.

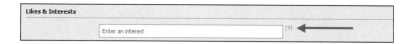

Just start typing a word, and suggestions appear in a list, where you can select them or just press Enter.

Then the interest appears in the box. If you like, you can click the X if you decide you don't want it.

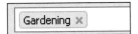

When you select an interest, it affects the number of people Facebook can send an ad to. (This is *targeting*). Evidently, nearly 1.5 million people on Facebook like gardening. Woohoo!

Next, click Continue.

Continue

The next screen is where you get a bit further into the nitty-gritty of online advertising. Again, you don't have to adjust much if you don't want to, with two major exceptions, indicated by the oversized arrows shown in Figure 14.5.

It's not a good idea to trust Facebook to have your best interests in mind on this screen unless you happen to be very wealthy.

It's a really, *really* good idea to make sure you adjust the budget and schedule. Otherwise, your bank account is eaten up at a rate of $50/day, until the end of time.

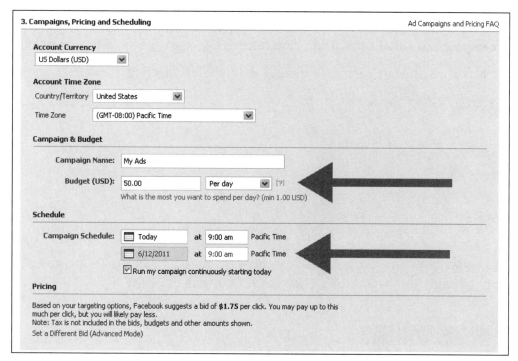

Figure 14.5
Make sure you are aware of the budget and schedule settings.

Unless you would like to give Facebook all your money, start by adjusting the budget to something like $10 a day.

And then, even more importantly, uncheck the Run My Campaign Continuously Starting Today check box.

Naughty, naughty Facebook.

Next, just as importantly, adjust the date range. No, I don't necessarily want an ad campaign to run a month into the future (although that is certainly okay).

Just be aware of what year, month, and date you're selecting.

To start, click on the date.

A calendar pops up. To go back and forward among months (remember, be aware of what year you're on), click the little triangles at the top.

Then click on the desired date.

Finally, it will look something like this. Ahhh, that's better.

Next, click on the Advanced Mode link.

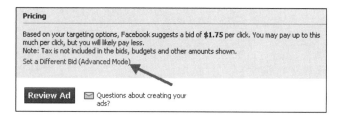

Facebook is happy to set a bid price for you on your ad.

If you develop an interest in online advertising, see the "Learning More About Facebook Advertising" section. Suffice it to say that with online ads, you can pay for a certain number of people to see the ad, called *impressions*, also associated with the term CPM. Or you can pay for each click; 1,000 people might see the ad, and maybe 4 people will click on it, and you pay per click. Starting out, the bid price on clicks is not necessarily what you'll pay; it's just that you *might* pay it. The pricing varies depending on how much competition there is for that interest/activity/particular demographic you're sending an ad to.

What I recommend, just to get started, is clicking that Advanced Mode link. Then enter in a Max Bid of $1.00. (Facebook automatically calculates a bid; in the next image, Facebook is suggesting $1.78.)

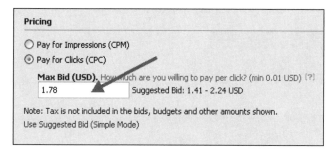

Click the Review Ad button.

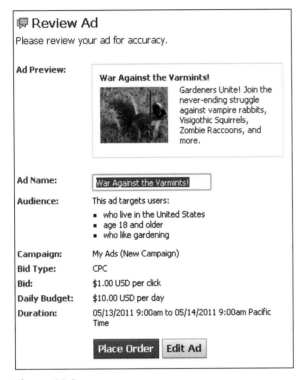

Take a look, edit the ad if you like (Edit Ad button), and then click the Place Order button (see Figure 14.6).

Figure 14.6
Reviewing the ad and placing the order.

Next, choose a funding source, and click the Okay button.

Enter in your credit card info, and click Submit (see Figure 14.7).

Enter Credit Card

Cardholder's First Name:

Cardholder's Last Name:

Credit Card Number:

VISA MasterCard AMERICAN EXPRESS DISCOVER JCB

Expiration Date: 05 ▾ 2011 ▾

Security Code (CSC):

What's a CSC?

Billing Address:

Billing Address 2:

City/Town:

State/Province/Region:

Zip/Postal Code:

Country: United States ▾

I have a coupon to redeem.

Submit Cancel

Figure 14.7
Entering in credit card info.

Facebook confirms that the credit card has been added to your account (which you can use for future ad campaigns), and you can click the Okay button.

Credit Card Added

The credit card has been added to your account.

Okay

Then you should see this Congratulations message.

Congratulations! You have just created your first ad.

Ads are grouped into campaigns, and we have automatically created the "My Ads" campaign for you. Ads in a campaign share a schedule and budget, which you can change from this page. When you create another ad, you will have the option to place it in an existing campaign or to create a new one.

Have a coupon code? **Add your coupon here.**

You see an overview of your ad campaign, as shown in Figure 14.8. Don't worry about all the individual particulars at the moment. See the "Learning More About Facebook Advertising" section in this chapter if you want to dig deeper.

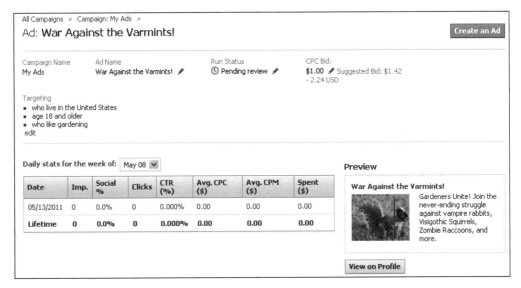

Figure 14.8
Basic high-level information. Initially ads are pending review; they start displaying when approved.

The most important thing to realize about this screen initially is that when you create your ad, it is pending review. Depending on the time of day, the day of the week, and the number of people Facebook has hired, it might take an hour for your ad to be reviewed/approved, or it might take a day. Until Facebook approves your ad, it doesn't run, and until it runs for a bit, you don't see information on this screen.

But at some point, you should get an email like this, which hopefully will announce your approval (see Figure 14.9).

Figure 14.9
An email confirming the approval of the ad.

ACCESSING ADS

To access your ads, go to www.facebook.com/ads/manage and log in if you aren't already.

You can select various settings on the side if you like.

A list of ads appears on the right, and you see the overall "campaign." (If you want to, you can make more than one ad for a given campaign to try different techniques and see which works best.)

To select an ad, click on its title.

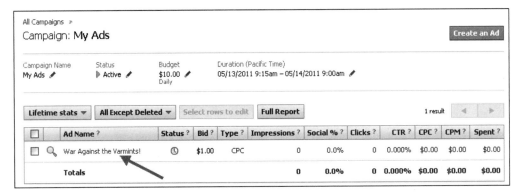

Also, when you're looking at ads on the campaign level, you can click on the little pencil by the status.

And you can pause it if you like.

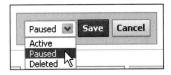

Then click Save.

MAKING AN AD FOR A FACEBOOK PAGE

Making a Facebook ad for a Facebook page is similar.

One thing you can do is visit your Facebook page and look down and to the right. Very likely, Facebook will show you how nice it would be to give it some money and make an ad (see Figure 14.10).

Figure 14.10
A sample ad may appear on your Facebook page.

To try out the sample ad, click on the Get More Likes button. (It might be Get More Fans or something else.)

When you get to the Design Your Ad screen, it prefills things such as the Destination drop-down menu (see Figure 14.11). It uses the title of your

Facebook page as the title for the ad, and it prefills whatever image you are using for your Facebook page. (You can click Browse to replace it.)

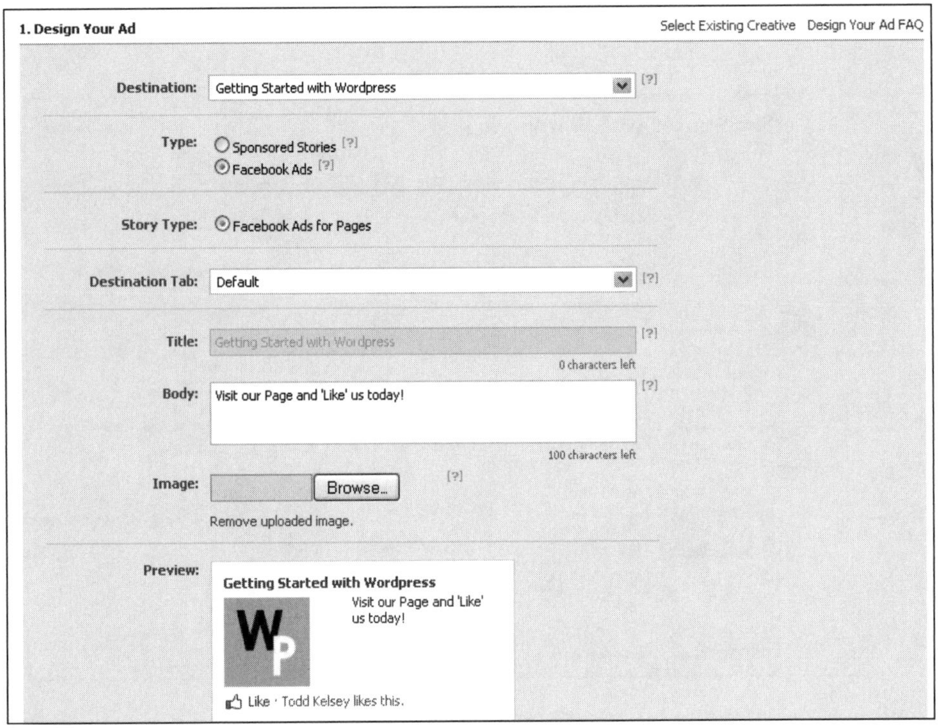

1. Design Your Ad   Select Existing Creative   Design Your Ad FAQ

Destination:	Getting Started with Wordpress ▼ [?]
Type:	○ Sponsored Stories [?] ◉ Facebook Ads [?]
Story Type:	◉ Facebook Ads for Pages
Destination Tab:	Default ▼ [?]
Title:	Getting Started with Wordpress [?] 0 characters left
Body:	Visit our Page and 'Like' us today! [?] 100 characters left
Image:	[Browse...] [?] Remove uploaded image.
Preview:	**Getting Started with Wordpress** Visit our Page and 'Like' us today! **W P** 👍 Like · Todd Kelsey likes this.

Figure 14.11
Some prefilled information for a potential ad.

The other way you can create an ad for a Facebook page is to go here:

http://www.facebook.com/advertising.

Click the Create an Ad button.

Then choose the desired Facebook page from the Destination drop-down menu.

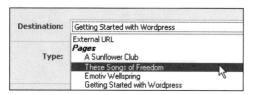

When you use this method, you may encounter a new thing Facebook has called Sponsored Stories. Feel free to read about it in the Facebook help section. We're going to focus on the ads. You can also click on the little question mark next to it.

Sponsored Stories tries to relate social activity or activity on the page to the ad. I prefer direct Facebook ads, but there would be no harm in trying a sponsored story and comparing the performance.

Because they are promoting Sponsored Stories, the screen may default to that setting.

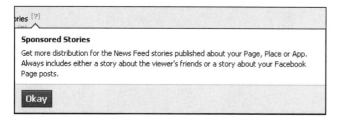

You can just click Facebook Ads.

You get the standard ad screen, where you can proceed as normal.

REVIEWING PERFORMANCE

After you've created your ad and it has been running, you'll want to see how things go.

If you're running an ad to a Facebook page, one way to see how things are going is to visit the page.

Here's a sample Facebook page, where I used an ad campaign to get Likes. It's not connected to a blog, but it's an example of developing social presence helped in part by Facebook ads (see Figure 14.12):

www.facebook.com/freedomsongs

The page was created to share a song meant to encourage protesters during the onset of the Middle East protests that shook things up. It was developed in English, and I tried using Google.com/translate to make some of the content available in Arabic and Farsi (Persian—Iran). I also used targeting to send the ads to various countries. It was a lot of fun.

Over time, the page has gathered some Likes. One technique for reviewing ad campaign performance is looking at how many Likes you end up with from week to week.

Figure 14.12
A sample page: keeping an eye on Likes to see how things are going.

One thing to celebrate is when you get 25 Likes, because then you can get a username. This means you go from the long link to your Facebook page to choosing a short descriptive name. Your page becomes www.facebook.com/ *username*.

Having 25 Likes creates a bit of momentum and might be a nice goal for an initial ad campaign. Then go to www.facebook.com/username and choose a name.

If you're lucky, the campaign will cost you $25 or less. Don't forget that you can tell all your Facebook friends about your page, too.

The other way to view performance for any kind of Facebook ad is to go to www. facebook.com/ads/manage.

Then click on the name of your Facebook campaign.

Don't worry too much about all the particulars.

In a nutshell, the Impressions are the number of people who may have seen the ad (not everyone looks at ads when they're on Facebook). Then you see how many people actually clicked on an ad.

This is at the campaign level. The CTR is the click-through rate, which is the percentage of people who saw the ad and clicked on it. Typical CTR for online advertising is quite low; only a small number of people click on any ad. But you can try different text and images and see which has a higher CTR. Then you can focus on that ad (and pause the others if you like).

When you click on the ad name (see previous graphic), you get more details.

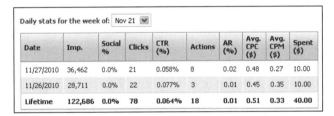

When you are running an ad for a Facebook page, the Actions column is the number of people who actually clicked on the Like button once they reached the page. So in the preceding example, 21 people clicked on the ad on 11/27, and 8 peopled Liked the page.

When you run an ad to your Facebook page, remember to put graphics, information, and a few posts on it. Ask yourself, "Would I click the Like button?"

Here's another example.

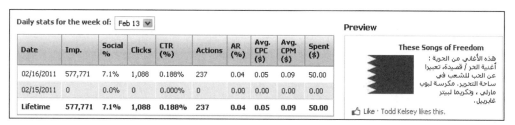

Another thing you can do is to click on the View Insights link on your Facebook page (when you are logged in).

It tells you information about Likes and includes some nifty graphs. To dig deeper, click See Details.

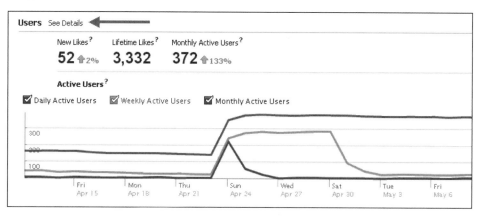

The details can be interesting (see Figure 14.13). Among other things, you can see a breakdown by gender and age group. In this case, you see some of the countries and cities that I ran ad campaigns to target for Facebook.com/freedomsongs. (Some of the exposure came from people sharing the page.)

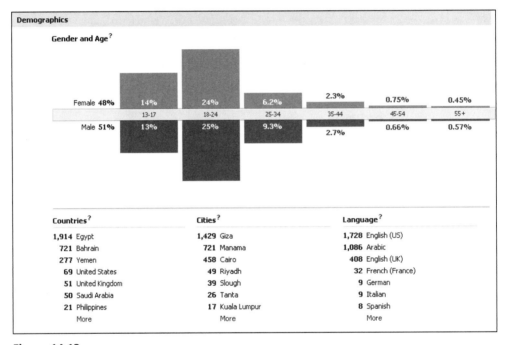

Figure 14.13
Interesting demographic information such as gender, countries, and language.

Starting a Revolution (or Helping One)

This is a small bonus section that simply relates a link to about a 10-minute video I made, describing the process of creating and running the ad campaign on Facebook for www.facebook.com/freedomsongs (see Figure 14.14).

To see the video, visit www.youtube.com/watch?v=WwfzaBOGHuA or http://tinyurl.com/fbadrevolution.

Figure 14.14
A YouTube video with some discussion on a sample Facebook advertising campaign.

LEARNING MORE ABOUT FACEBOOK ADVERTISING

To learn more about Facebook advertising, visit ww.facebook.com/adsmarketing/ (see Figure 14.15).

There's a lot of good information that you can dig into.

If you would like to read a book, search for Facebook advertising primer on Amazon. If you have a Kindle and would like to visit, head to www.facebookadvertisingprimer.com, where you can purchase a PDF copy.

And if you'd like to read a book but can't afford to buy one, visit www.facebookadvertisingprimer.com/chapters.

I just didn't give out that link, and we didn't have this conversation. Har, har.

(Don't worry; I wrote the book, and I like the idea of sharing it for free if need be.)

Woohoo!

Figure 14.15
Guide to Facebook Ads.

INVESTIGATING OTHER KINDS OF SOCIAL ADVERTISING

There's more to social advertising than just Facebook ads. You might be interested in investigating www.mashable.com or www.socialmediaexaminer.com to learn more about the world of social media; both are good sites.

Other forms of getting exposure could involve creating a Twitter account and making a tweet whenever you post to your blog.

Or if your blog is particularly business related, you might like to investigate creating a LinkedIn group and posting information there, or joining some groups and making mention of your blog on those groups. (You also might like to add a link to your blog on your LinkedIn profile. Ding ding ding.)

Depending on your interests and budget, you might want to investigate trying a Google ad. I used to be intimidated by Google AdWords because it felt too wizardy. But after making a Facebook ad, I thought I'd try it. Having a Google ad can be another way to get some traffic and a good learning experience. To learn more about AdWords, visit www.google.com/adwords, or see www.cftwpress.com/tutorials for an entire free book I wrote on learning about it.

There's an interesting program called Google Grants, where under the right conditions, 501(c)3 organizations can get free advertising, up to $120,000.00 a year's worth! See the AdWords tutorials at www.cftwpress.com/tutorials or visit www.google.com/grants. (And if you need some help, drop me a line at tekelsey@gmail.com.)

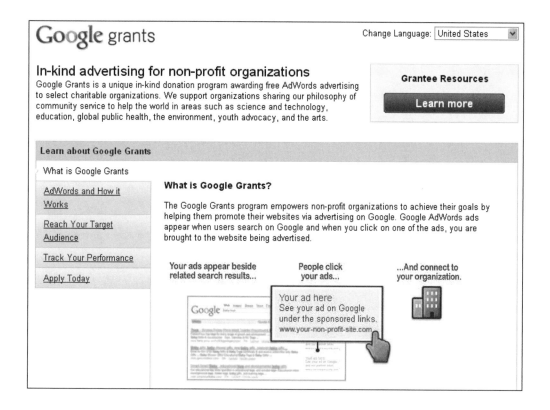

Conclusion

Dear Reader,

Congratulations on taking a look at social advertising. The best way to get started is just to try it; don't worry about all the details. I'm confident there's a reasonable chance that you will have enough fun creating an ad that you might try it again. And again.

Best wishes!

Regards,

Todd

CHAPTER 15

A FEW SAMPLE BLOGS

In This Chapter:

- Tour Stop #1: www.juntaedelane.com
- Tour Stop #2: Digital Days
- Tour Stop #3: Brotherhood of the Briar

This chapter is courtesy of guest writer Mark Neal.

It's time to take a break from building your own blog and take a look at what a few people have done with WordPress. In this chapter, we'll review some things to consider as you learn about WordPress. So hop on the tour bus, fasten your seatbelt, and enjoy the ride.

TOUR STOP #1: WWW.JUNTAEDELANE.COM

Juntae DeLane is an advertising, marketing, and social media strategist. His site reflects his engagement and work with emerging media and his goal to promote himself as an emerging marketing consultant. Check out www.juntaedelane. com/.

Figure 15.1 shows the front page of Juntae's site.

The site design uses top-level navigation with posts updated on the left side of the page while the right side of the page remains static. It's a simple, straightforward, and uncluttered design.

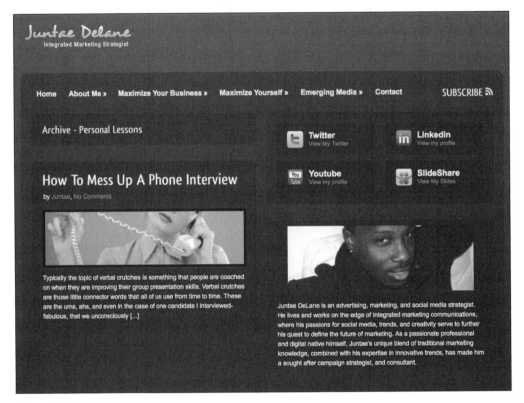

Figure 15.1
Juntae DeLane's WordPress site.

One of the things Juntae does well is make several social media buttons prominent on the static part of his site so others can see his activity on those sites with a simple click.

To promote his site and drive traffic to it, Juntae utilizes Facebook, Twitter, and LinkedIn and tries to post to the blog two or three times a month. He has also connected Google Analytics to his site to keep track of traffic sources as well as the engagement level of those visiting. His strategy is to post relevant content that is interesting to those who want to explore emerging media to stimulate conversation to keep people coming back.

For example, the following post looks at the pros and cons of Twitter and Facebook and uses an image to get attention (see Figure 15.2).

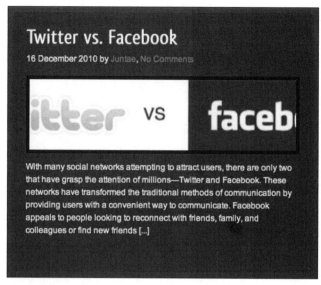

Figure 15.2
A blog post showing relevant content.

Juntae created a *blogroll*, which is a list of links to other blogs (see Figure 15.3). This makes it easy for users to get quick access to related sites without having to search for them.

Figure 15.3
A list of links, called a blogroll.

Another nice feature is the way Juntae's Twitter account updates right on the front page of his site, so visitors can see his most recent tweets (see Figure 15.4).

Figure 15.4
A Twitter update option preloaded into a theme.

This is another way to build content and interaction into a blog. This Twitter option comes preloaded with the theme that Juntae chose from www. woothemes.com/.

Juntae Recommends: Use themes to enhance the appearance of your site.

Tour Stop #2: Digital Days

Elisa King is a student in the Digital Marketing Communications Program at West Virginia University. She started her blog for a class assignment, and all her entries currently involve posts about digital/social media (see Figure 15.5). Her blog is called Digital Days and can be viewed at http://elisathinks. wordpress.com.

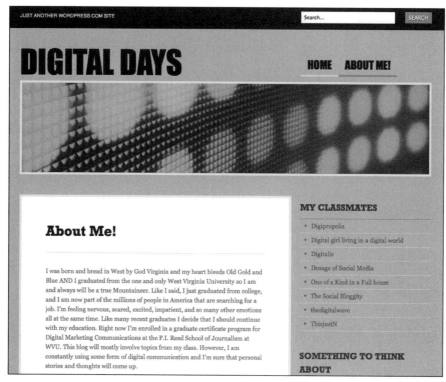

Figure 15.5
Elisa King's blog, Digital Days.

The blog has a simple and compact design. It's organized well, so there's no stumbling around wondering where to find the information you need.

Elisa's blog is a great example of an effective layout. She's used what WordPress calls a *custom header*, which is basically just a large photo at the top of the page. There's some top- and side-level navigation, and her posts update on the left side of the page, while the right side remains static.

Elisa has used the paid theme service www.woothemes.com/. It allows you to upload different themes with some increased functionality.

Elisa currently posts once or twice a week and has a blogroll and some other links for general interest (see Figure 15.6).

Figure 15.6
An example of a blogroll.

At the bottom of her site, Elisa has a place for users to subscribe (see Figure 15.7). This is simply a widget that she used from WordPress.

Figure 15.7
A WordPress subscription widget.

If you already have a WordPress account, when you click the Sign Me Up button and enter an email associated with that account, WordPress subscribes you through that account, where you can also manage your subscriptions. If you don't have a WordPress account, just enter your email address. Once you click on the link in the email that is sent to you to activate your subscription, you see a page like Figure 15.8.

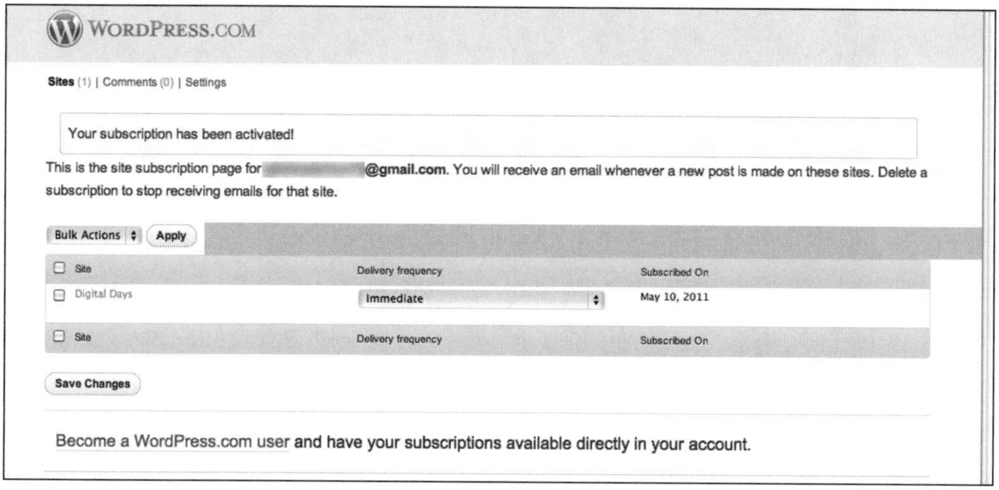

Figure 15.8
A subscription management Dashboard.

From this page, you can manage subscriptions to whatever blogs you have through WordPress. For example, you can delete a subscription or specify how often you want updates to be delivered. It would be a good idea to bookmark this page so you have quick access to it.

Elisa enjoys WordPress and finds it easy to use. Even though she considers herself a beginner, she is having fun expressing her opinion and creating her own material.

For example, one of her blog posts looks at a product called the Snuggie and shows how it "went viral" or gained recognition through video parodies of the original infomercial (see Figure 15.9).

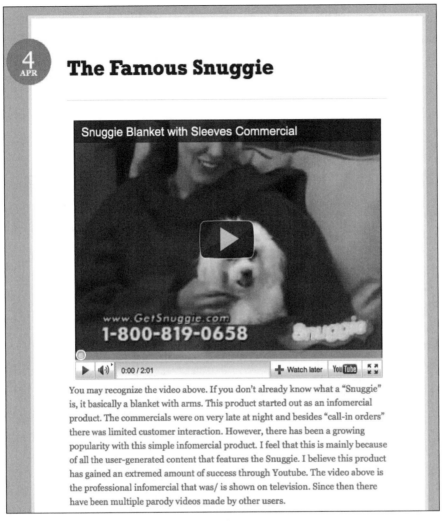

Figure 15.9
An example of a video post.

One nice thing Elisa does is incorporate a number of videos into her post. Videos are one way to create greater engagement with an audience and keep them coming back to a blog.

Elisa Recommends: Have fun! WordPress is easy to use, so exercise your creativity.

TOUR STOP #3: BROTHERHOOD OF THE BRIAR

Let's look at one more blog. The Brotherhood of the Briar blog uses the free version of WordPress, shown in Figure 15.10. It's my own site that I created to have some fun with a group of friends who get together every Thursday night to smoke pipes and have conversation around a fire. See http://markneal.wordpress.com.

Figure 15.10
Brotherhood of the Briar blog.

One thing I am big on when it comes to blogging is design. I believe that a big factor in whether people stay at your blog once they've landed there is how attractive it is and how easy it is to navigate. Is it too distracting or busy? Is there not enough information or is it not easily located? I want my readers to be able to quickly navigate and find what they need.

What I've done with Brotherhood of the Briar is tried to create an atmosphere on the blog that reflects in some way the Thursday night gatherings, which always take place outside around a fire at a college professor's home. So I chose a dark theme and some photos of logs and a fire. I like the fact that the free version of WordPress has a range of themes to choose from.

I'm a big fan of the custom header in the free WordPress version; I used a custom photo that stretches across the top of the blog. In this case, it's a number of logs in my garage waiting to be split. Visitors see the header first. If it's attractive or intriguing, they might explore further.

I also try to have highly organized, easy-to-use navigation. All of my navigation is in the sidebar on the right. I've added a widget or module called Categories that I've found useful for organizing posts into subject groups. When users click on the Chronicles from the Brotherhood of the Briar link, they are taken to a page where they can scroll through all the posts there (see Figure 15.11).

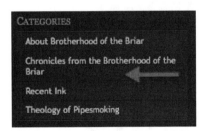

Figure 15.11
Easy navigation: categories and links.

A little further down on my sidebar, I chose to add a Recent Comments widget (see Figure 15.12).

Figure 15.12
A Recent Comments widget.

This widget lets visitors see right away that there has been some interaction on my blog. In theory, this sort of visible engagement might increase the chances that other people will interact or comment on my blog. I try to respond to every comment I get. I do occasionally get spam, but Akismet spam blocker blocks most of it.

I haven't promoted Brotherhood of the Briar on social networks, but I have encouraged people to subscribe to the blog so they can get automatic updates. I've placed this widget prominently at the top of my sidebar with options to subscribe via email or RSS (really simple syndication) feed (see Figure 15.13).

Figure 15.13
A subscription widget.

I was primarily interested in the design of the blog; making it look good and be functional and easy to navigate. I didn't necessarily want to promote it to a large audience, as it would really only make sense to people who were part of the group. However, as part of your strategy to create engagement and drive traffic to your blog, I highly recommend using this widget and placing it in a prominent postion on your site.

Another thing I would recommend is enabling some kind of "share" function at the bottom of each post. (For the hosted version of WordPress, see Chapter 11, "Easy Expansion: Integrating Facebook and GTranslate," or search in plugins for share buttons.) In the free version of WordPress, you can find this under Settings > Sharing on your Dashboard. This way, if people really like a post, they can quickly share it on Facebook, Twitter, or wherever.

One way to engage people is to use lots of photos. Most people don't like to be confronted with only a wall of text, so add some photos! I like to take my own and then upload them to WordPress (see Figure 15.14). One alternative is to get public domain photos from a site like http://publicdomainpictures.net/.

Figure 15.14
An example of a post with a photo.

Just for fun, I've also added a tag cloud widget to the sidebar (see Figure 15.15).

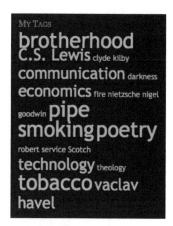

Figure 15.15
A tag cloud widget.

A *tag cloud* is a list of different tags, or subjects, used to label a blog post based on what it's about. The size of the word in a tag cloud gets bigger the more that tag is used to label different posts. A user could simply click on one of the words in the cloud and be taken to a list of posts that have been tagged with that word. A tag cloud offers a quick way to see what kinds of things are being written about in a blog.

Mark Recommends: Look at your site design. Think about the people visiting your site, and put yourself in their place. What would you want to see? What would make it easy for them to get around? What would make your site attractive? Experiment. Don't be afraid to ask people for their opinion while you are designing your blog. This effective strategy is called *usability testing*. Most of all, have fun!

CONCLUSION

Dear Reader,

Thanks for taking this travel tour of a few WordPress blogs, courtesy of guest writer Mark Neal. We've seen a few examples of the kinds of things other people are trying. Hopefully it's given you some ideas of things *you* can try.

Congratulations on making it through the entire book!

Regards,

Todd

P.S. Feel free to submit your blog or any links you've found helpful to the Facebook page www.facebook.com/pages/WordPress-Primer/186134644744074 or http://tinyurl.com/wpp-fb.

INDEX

A

About link, 197
accessing
 categories, 147
 Dashboard (Blogger), 52–53
 Facebook ads, 281–282
 Google Analytics, 178–180
 pages, 195–201
 related posts, 228
 RSS Graffiti Facebook
  application, 264
 Settings page, 223
 site visits, 166. *See also*
  statistics
 widgets, 206
accounts
 AdWords, 92. *See also*
  AdWords
 blogs
  fee-based, 38
  starting, 41–50
 Control Panel, 87
 Gmail, 171
 Google, 96, 173. *See also*
  Google
 hosting, starting, 84–87
 passwords, 44
 setup
  Blogger, 22–35
  Gmail, 21–22
 statistics, 164
Activate Plugin link, 149, 205
activating. *See also* **starting**
 emails, 45
 Google Analytics, 170

**Add a Forwarding Address
 button, 21**
Add an Image window, 60–61
Add button, 229
Ad Design section, 270
Add Feed button, 262
adding
 applications, 258
 borders, 75
 captions, 61, 63
 categories, 143
 features, 131
 feeds, 262
 images, 29–32, 55, 198
  from Facebook, 67–69
  to posts, 136
 links, 253
 pages, 195–201
 plugins, Facebook, 204–208
 profiles, 175
 tags, 229–230
 themes, 185–195. *See also*
  themes
 video, 231–236
 widgets, 11
 YouTube videos, 231–234
Add Media Files window, 54
Add New button, 114, 196, 204
**Add New Category button,
 142–143**
Add New Page feature, 196
addresses, 5
 Add a Forwarding Address
  button, 21
 availability of, checking, 25

 Blogger, 18–19
 blogs, 24
 email. *See also* email
 fee-based blogs, 37
 feeds, 263
 Forward a Copy of Incoming
  Mail, 22
 Gmail, 94. *See also* Gmail
 IP (Internet Protocol), 106
Add RSS Graffiti button, 260
adjusting. *See* **modifying**
administration
 QuickInstall, 90
 Site Admin link, 53
Admin Page link, 149
ads
 Facebook
  accessing, 281–282
  creating, 269–281
  managing, 283–286
  resources, 291–292
  reviewing performance,
   286–290
  running campaigns,
   290–291
 selecting, 282
Advanced Edit mode, 73
advantages
 of Blogger, 20
 of Facebook, 8–11
advertising, 7. *See also*
 promoting
 social, promoting with,
  267–294
 Twitter, 292–294

AdWords, 92
    credit, redeeming, 93–99
    payment options, 99
AdWords Primer, 92
Akismet, 107–111
All in One SEO Pack, 148–150
Allow button, 258, 262
alternate text, images, 61
Amazon, 291
Analytics. *See* Google Analytics
APIs (application programming
    interfaces), 164
    WP-reCAPTCHA plugin, 237
Appearance button, 124, 185.
    See also themes
application programming
    interfaces. *See* APIs
applications
    adding, 258
    authorizing, 257
    RSS Graffiti Facebook,
        248–249
        accessing, 264
        installing, 256–264
applying special effects to
    images, 75
Apps icon, 253
archives, 4
art, selling, 15
assigning numbers to pages, 201
associating posts, 145
audiences, targeting, 272–274
authorizing
    applications, 257
    Facebook, 259
authors, multiple author blogs, 8
automating
    backups, 116. *See also* backups
    default settings, 229
availability of addresses,
    checking, 25
Available Themes, 194. *See also*
    themes

B

Backup link, 116
Back Up Now button, 116

backups, 102–103, 112–113.
    See also security
Backup tool, 116
BackupWordPress, 113–117
Backup Your Database and Files
    link, 112
basic configurations, 130–134
Before a Comment Appears
    section, 106
Billing Preferences option
    (AdWords), 98
blocking spam, 107–111.
    See also spam
BlogBooker, 103, 118–121
Blogger, 11–13, 17–18
    account setup, 22–35
    navigating, 18–20
    templates, 26
blogrolls, 4, 297, 299
blogs
    accounts, starting, 41–50
    backups, 112–113
    Blogger. *See* Blogger
    Facebook
        connecting, 252–264
        promoting on, 249–251
        sharing on, 56–58
    fee-based, selecting, 37–40
    free
        selecting, 37–40
        starting, 37–58
    images, adding, 29–32
    importing, 253
    multiple, 38–40
    naming, 19, 24
    New Post button, 50–52
    overview of, 3–8
    posting, 27–29, 32–35,
        134–138. *See also* posting
    previewing, 263
    privacy, selecting, 48–50
    profiles, importing,
        248–249, 265
    public, selecting, 48–50
    publishing, 28
    restoring, 117
    sample, 295–308
    subscribing, 250

updating, 111–112
    video, adding, 231–236
    viewing, 249
Blog Software section, 88
bookmarks
    AdWords, 93
    Dashboard (Blogger), 91
    passwords, 47
    QuickInstall, 87
borders, adding, 75
Brotherhood of the Briar blog,
    303–307
Browse button, 114, 127
browsers
    interfaces. *See* interfaces
    plugins, 220
    Remember Password bar, 47
budgets, online advertising, 274

C

cafepress.com, 15
campaigns, 282. *See also*
    promoting
captions
    adding, 63
    images, 61
Cascading Style Sheets. *See* CSS
Categories
    feature, 142–147
    panels, 144
    widgets, 133–134, 196, 304
categories, 4, 147, 230
categorizing
    posts, 144–146
    uncategorized posts, 146–147
cell phones, 265
    portability, 86
Choose File button, 272
Click Here to Add RSS Graffiti
    button
Click Here to Authorize RSS
    Graffiti button, 258
Click Here to Fetch and Preview
    It link, 263
Click to Authorize button, 261
Close link, 207
cloud tags, 307

code
Google Analytics, 176–177
SEO (search engine
optimization), 156–158
**Comment Blacklist
function, 107**
**Comment Moderation
function, 107**
**Comment Moderation
setting, 106**
comments, 6
Leave a Comment link, 6
Other Comment Settings, 106
spam, 102
modifying settings,
104–107
overview of, 103–104
WP-reCAPTCHA plugin,
237–241
commerce, 15
configuring
basic configurations, 130–134
Facebook
ads, 269–281
plugins, 204–208
FeedBurner, 221
Google Analytics, 169–183
GTranslate, 210–215
statistics, 161–168
widgets, 224
WP e-Commerce plugin,
241–244
WP-reCAPTCHA plugin,
237–241
Yet Another Related Posts
plugin, 226–231
confirmation messages
Akismet, 111
BackupWordPress, 115
Google Analytics, 170
GTranslate, 211
Notes feature, 255
plugins, 205
quick installations, 90
SEO (search engine
optimization), 149
statistics, 163
themes, 188

Confirm button, 249
**connecting blogs to Facebook
pages, 252–264.** *See also* **links**
**contact information,
Akismet, 110**
Continue button, 71, 89, 109
Control Panel, 87
copying
links into Facebook, 248
passwords, 47
videos, 232
costs, 12–13
hosting, 84
online advertising, 274
selecting sources, 278
cPanel Login, 87–88
Create an Ad button, 269, 284
Create Page button, 250
Create tab, 74
**Create Your Blog Now
button, 24**
**credit, redeeming AdWords,
93–99**
credit card info, entering, 279
cropping images, 126–127
CSS (Cascading Style Sheets), 66
currency, 97. *See also* **costs**
**Current Theme,
modifying, 193**
customizing
addresses, 19
basic configurations, 130–134
Blogger, 20
blogs, 5
design, 12
Facebook
ads, 269–281
plugins, 204–208
Google Analytics, 169–183
GTranslate, 210–215
images, 31, 60–67
headers, 128, 299
with picnik.com, 73–76
resizing, 72
statistics, 161–168
themes, 124–129, 185–195
WP e-Commerce plugin,
241–244

**WP-reCAPTCHA plugin,
237–241**
**Yet Another Related Posts
plugin, 226–231**

D
Dashboard
Blogger, 23
accessing, 52–53
links, 47–48
WordPress
bookmarks, 91
enabling, 180–183
statistics, 168
dates, Google Analytics, 179
deactivating Akismet, 111
default settings
Ad Design section, 270
automated, 229
**descriptions of images, entering,
61–62**
design, 5, 12
Design Your Ad screen, 270, 283
Destination menu, 270–271, 285
developers, hiring, 13–15
development, 13–15
devices, mobile, 265
Digital Days blog, 298–302
digital images, 59–80. *See also*
images
disadvantages
of Blogger, 20
of Facebook, 8–11
Discussion link, 105
documents
PDF (Portable Document
Format), 120–121
WP e-Commerce, 241–244
domains
names, 42. *See also* naming
subdomains, 90
WP-reCAPTCHA plugin, 239
Donate button, 120
Download button, 113
**Download Export File
button, 119**
downloading images, 126

Download link, 117
dragging
    GTranslate, 212
    widgets, 206
dropping widgets, 206

E

ecommerce, 241–244
Edit Ad button, 278
editing. *See also* modifying
    Advanced Edit mode, 73
    Facebook pages, 252
    images, 64, 126
    links, 198
    options, 75
    pages, 197–198
    picnik.com, 73–76
    Quick Edit, 201
    titles, 230
Edit link, 147
Edit Page link, 252
Edit Settings link, 253
effects, special, 71
elisathinks.wordpress.com,
    298–302
email. *See also* Gmail
    activation, 45
    Forward a Copy of Incoming
        Mail, 22
    lists, subscribing to, 221–226
Embed button, 235
embedding
    video manually, 235
    YouTube videos, 231–234
empty feeds, 263. *See also*
    feeds
Empty the Page Cache
    button, 115
Enabled button, 150
Enable Subscribe2 Widget, 223
enabling
    Dashboard (WordPress),
        180–183
    thumbnails, 78
English, 215. *See also* languages
entering
    credit card info, 279

passwords, 46
promotion codes,
    AdWords, 99
exporting BlogBooker, 119
External URL, 270

F

Facebook, 7
    ads
        accessing, 281–282
        creating, 269–281
        managing, 283–286
        resources, 291–292
        reviewing performance,
            286–290
        running campaigns, 290–291
    advantages/disadvantages of,
        8–11
    authorizing, 259
    blogs
        connecting, 252–264
        promoting on, 249–251
        sharing on, 32–35, 56–58
    editing, 252
    help, 285
    images, posting, 67–69
    Like button, 209
    links, copying into, 248
    plugins, 204–208
    RSS Graffiti Facebook
        application, 248–249
        accessing, 264
        installing, 256–264
    SEO (search engine
        optimization), 159–160
    sharing on, 215–217
Featured themes, 188
Feature Filter, 186
features, 3–8
    adding, 131
    Categories, 142–147
fee-based blogs, selecting, 37–40
FeedBurner, 221
feeds
    adding, 262
    addresses, 263
fees, 12–13, 84

File Manager, 116
filenames, 78. *See also* naming
files, Add Media Files
    window, 54
Fill Light feature (Picasa), 77
Find Themes button, 186
Firefox, 21, 47
formatting
    BackupWordPress, 113–117
    basic configurations, 130–134
    blogs, 27–29
    captions, 61
    categories, 143
    Facebook
        ads, 269–281
        plugins, 204–208
    Google Analytics, 169–183
    GTranslate, 210–215
    images, 60–67
    passwords, 44
    posts, 135
    SEO (search engine
        optimization), 150
    statistics, 161–168
    themes, 124–129, 185–195
    titles, 27
    widgets, 224
    WP e-Commerce plugin,
        241–244
    WP-reCAPTCHA plugin,
        237–241
    Yet Another Related Posts
        plugin, 226–231
Forward a Copy of Incoming
    Mail, 22
forwarding, Add a Forwarding
    Address button, 21
free blogs
    selecting, 37–40
    starting, 37–58
funding. *See* costs

G

general settings, 130–134
Get More Likes button, 283
Get Started Now button, 88
Get Your Key Here link, 163

Get Your Key link, 108
Gmail, 11
    accounts, 171
    AdWords, 94
    setup, 21–22
    WP-reCAPTCHA plugin, 238
Google
    AdWords, 92–99, 293
    Analytics, 169–183
        accessing, 178–180
        bringing code back into,
            176–177
        returning to, 174–176
    Gmail. *See* Gmail
    Grants, 293
    keywords, 152
Grant Access button, 182
Grants (Google), 293
graphics, 29–32. *See also* images
groups, LinkedIn, 292

H
header images
    choosing, 128
    customizing, 299
Header link, 125
help, Facebook, 285
High Quality area, 234
hiring developers, 13–15
Home Description link, 152
Home Title link, 151
hostgator.com, 12, 92
hosting
    accounts, starting, 84–87
    fee-based blogs, 38
    one-click installation, 83–100
HTML (Hypertext Markup
    Language), 66

I
images
    adding, 29–32, 198
    Add Media Files window, 54
    ads, 272
    borders, adding, 75
    cropping, 126–127
    editing with picnik.com, 73–76

Facebook, posting, 67–69
    headers, customizing, 299
    importing, 76
    managing with Picasa, 76–77
    optimizing, 60–67
    posting, 52–56, 63, 136
    renaming, 77–79
    resizing from picresize.com,
        70–73
    saving, 75–76, 127
    scanning, 76, 271
    sizing, 65
    special effects, applying, 75
    themes, 125
    uploading, 126
    URLs (uniform resource
        locators), 62
importing
    blogs, 253
    images, 76
    profiles, 248–249, 265
impressions, 277
inserting images, 55
installing
    Akismet, 107–108
    BackWordPress plugin, 114
    FeedBurner, 221
    Google Analytics, 169–170
    one-click installation,
        83–100
    QuickInstall, 87–92
    RSS Graffiti Facebook
        application, 256–264
    SEO (search engine
        optimization), 148
    statistics, 162
    themes, 125, 188
    WP e-Commerce plugin,
        241–244
    Yet Another Related Posts
        plugin, 227
Install link, 162
Install Now button, 115
interfaces. *See also* browsers
    APIs (application
        programming
        interfaces), 164
    Firefox, 21

intimidation, getting over
    (social advertising), 268–269
IP (Internet Protocol)
    addresses, 106
istockphoto.com, 271

J–K
juntadelane.com, 295–298

keys
    Akismet, 108, 110
    CAPTCHA, 239
keywords, 152
Kindle, 291

L
languages, GTranslate, 210–215
Leave a Comment link, 6
Like a Facebook page, 250
Like button, Facebook, 209
LinkedIn, 292
links, 7
    About, 197
    Activate Plugin, 149, 205
    adding, 253
    Admin Page, 149
    Backup, 116
    Backup Your Database and
        Files, 112
    blogs to Facebook pages,
        252–264
    categories, 146
    Click Here to Fetch and
        Preview It, 263
    Close, 207
    Dashboard (Blogger), 47–48
    Discussion, 105
    Download, 117
    Edit, 147
    editing, 198
    Edit Page, 252
    Edit Settings, 253
    Facebook, copying into, 248
    Get Your Key, 108
    Get Your Key Here, 163
    Header, 125
    Home Description, 152

links (*Continued*)
Home Title, 151
images, URLs (uniform
resource locators), 62
Leave a Comment, 6
Pages, 195
pasting, 233
Preview, 187
privacy, 49
Restoring, 117
search-engine-friendly URLs,
158–159
Settings, 130
Sign Up, 108
Site Admin, 53
Upload, 114
View Insights, 289
View Page, 197, 199
View Post, 51, 137
View Report, 178
youtube.com, 232
lists
email, subscribing, 221–226
pages, 200
of plugins, 205
Load Live Preview button, 71
Log In link, 91
logs, Categories, 142
Lussier, Oliver, 205

M

magazines, online, 8
Manage Themes tab, 125
managing
Facebook ads, 283–286
features, 131
File Manager, 116
images with Picasa, 76–77
multiple blogs, 38–40
quick installations, 88
Site Admin link, 53
themes, 125
Manual Backup area, 117
manually embedding video, 235
markneal.wordpress.com,
302–307
Max Bids, 277

menus, Resize Your Picture, 71
messages
BlogBooker, 119
confirmation
Akismet, 111
BackupWordPress, 115
Google Analytics, 170
GTranslate, 211
Notes feature, 255
plugins, 205
SEO (search engine
optimization), 149
statistics, 163
themes, 188
email. *See* email
status, 115
you can get the keys here,
238
You may manage your
subscription options,
225
meta, 4
mobile devices, 265
modifying
comments, 104–107
Current Theme, 193
dates, Google Analytics, 179
images, 60–67, 70–73
posts after publishing, 138
widgets, 192, 208–210
Modify Picture panel, 73
monetizing, 7
moving
GTranslate, 212
images, 31
widgets, 132, 206
multiple author blogs, 8
multiple blogs, 38–40
Multi-User, WordPress, 38–40

N

nameservers, 86
naming
blogs, 19, 24
categories, 142
fee-based blogs, 37
images, 60, 77–79

subdomains, 90
usernames, selecting,
41–42, 287
navigating
BlogBooker, 118–121
Blogger, 18–20
blogs, 3–8
plugins, 220
Settings area, 105
themes, 185–195
New Account Signup
area, 172
New Post button, 50–52,
135, 144
News Feed, 57
News theme, 188
Normal Mode area, 234
Notes feature, 253–255
Notes icon, 254
numbers, assigning pages, 201

O

Okay button, 254, 278
one-click installation,
83–100
online advertising, 267–294
online magazines, 8
open source software, 221
optimizing images, 60–67
options. *See also* customizing
AdWord payments, 99
Billing Preferences option
(AdWords), 98
Facebook
ads, 269–281
plugins, 204–208
Google Analytics, 169–183
images, 60–67
picresize.com, 71
quick installations, 89
renaming, 78
resizing, 71
statistics, 165
subscribing, 226
themes, 185–195
WP e-Commerce plugin,
241–244

WP-reCAPTCHA plugin,
    237–241
Yet Another Related Posts
    plugin, 226–231
Other Comment Settings, 106

P
pages
    adding, 195–201
    Facebook. *See* Facebook
    lists, 200
    numbers, assigning, 201
Pages link, 195
panels
    Categories, 144
    Post Tags, 229
parent categories, 143
passwords
    entering, 46
    formatting, 44
    QuickInstall, 87, 90
    Remember Password bar, 47
pasting links, 233
payments, AdWords options, 99.
    See also **costs**
PDF (Portable Document
    Format) documents, 120–121
performance, reviewing
    Facebook ads, 286–290
Personal Site section, 108
phones, cell, 265
Picasa, managing images with,
    76–77
picnik.com, editing images with,
    73–76
picresize.com, resizing images,
    70–73
pictures, 29–32. *See also* **images**
pixels, 72
Place Order button, 278
plugins, 12, 43, 219
    Akismet, 107–111
    BackupWordPress, 113–117
    Blogger, 11
    browsing, 220
    email lists, subscribing to,
        221–226
    Facebook, 204–208

Google Analytics, 169–183
GTranslate, 210–215
SEO (search engine
    optimization), 148–158
Share, 215–217
Smart YouTube, 231–234
statistics, 161–168
themes, 188. *See also* themes
WP e-Commerce, 241–244
WP-reCAPTCHA, 237–241
Yet Another Related Posts,
    226–231
portability, cell phones, 86
positioning images, 31
posting, 134–138
    blogs, 27–29
        on Facebook, 57
        sharing on Facebook, 32–35
    categorizing, 144–146
    images, 52–56, 63, 67–69
    modifying after
        publishing, 138
    New Post button, 50–52
    SEO (search engine
        optimization), 153–156
    uncategorized posts,
        categorizing, 146–147
    video, adding, 231–236
Post Tags panel, 229
preferences
    Billing Preferences option
        (AdWords), 98
    zones, 97
prefilling
    information for ads, 284
    usernames, 43
preinstalled images, 128
previewing
    ads, 271
    blogs, 263
    posts, 137
    themes, 188
Preview link, 187
price sliders, 109
pricing. *See* **costs**
Primary Widget area, 131, 133,
    207, 224
Primary widget area, 192
privacy, selecting blogs, 48–50

private keys, 239
profiles
    adding, 175
    blogs, importing, 248–249, 265
    LinkedIn, 292
    viewing, 178
    websites, 172
promoting
    blogs on Facebook, 249–251
    RSS Graffiti Facebook
        application, 248–249
    with social advertising,
        267–294
    on social media, 247–266
promotion codes, AdWords, 99
public blogs, selecting, 48–50
publicdomainpictures.net, 271
public keys, 239
Publish button, 137, 145,
    236, 255
publishing
    blogs, 28
    images, 56, 127
    videos, 233. *See also* videos
purchasing. *See also* **costs**
    hosting services, 84–85
    online advertising, 274

Q–R
Quick Edit, 201
QuickInstall, 87–92

ranges, modifying dates, 179
reading comments, 6
Really Simple Syndication
    (RSS), 305
rearranging features, 131
redeeming credit, Google
    AdWords, 93–99
reducing spam, 107–111.
    See also **spam**
Referrers section, 167
Refresh button, 131
register.com, 86
registering
    AdWords, 95–96
    fee-based blogs, 38
Remember Password bar, 47

renaming images, 77–79
reports
  Google Analytics, 180. *See also*
    Google, Analytics
  View Report link, 178
Resize Your Picture menu, 71
resizing
  images from picresize.com,
    70–73
  options, 71
resources, Facebook ads,
291–292
restoring blogs, 117. *See also*
  backups
Restoring link, 117
returning to Google Analytics,
174–176
Review Ad button, 278
reviewing performance,
  Facebook ads, 286–290
right-clicking, images to
  download, 126
RSS (Really Simple
  Syndication), 305
RSS Graffiti Facebook
  application, 248–249
  accessing, 264
  installing, 256–264
Run My Campaign
  Continuously Starting Today
  check box, 275
running Facebook ad
  campaigns, 290–291

S
sales, 15
  e-commerce, 241–244
sample blogs, 295–308
  Brotherhood of the Briar,
    303–307
  Digital Days, 298–302
  juntadelane.com, 295–298
Save button, 134, 192, 207, 263
Save Changes button, 130, 213
saving
  images, 75–76, 127
  passwords, 44

scanning images, 76, 271
scheduling Facebook
  advertising, 274–275
search-engine-friendly URLs,
  158–159
search engine optimization. *See*
  SEO
search engines, listing on, 12
searching
  Facebook plugins, 205, 216
  plugins, 220
  themes, 186
Search Plugins button, 148, 162
Search widget, 133
security, 101–102
  Akismet, 107–111
  backups, 112–113
  BackupWordPress, 113–117
  comments, modifying settings,
    104–107
  overview of, 102–104
  passwords, selecting, 44
  spam. *See* spam
  updating WordPress,
    111–112
Select Files button, 54, 60
selecting
  ads, 282
  blogs
    privacy, 48–50
    public, 48–50
  fee-based blogs, 37–40
  free blogs, 37–40
  parents, 143
  passwords, 44
  plugins, 220
  templates, 26
  themes, 124–129
  usernames, 41–42, 287
  videos, 232
SEO (search engine
  optimization), 141,
  148–158, 268
  code, 156–158
  Facebook, 159–160
  posting, 153–156
SEOBook, 153
SEO Made Simple, 153

servers, nameservers, 86
settings
  basic configurations, 130–134
  comments, modifying,
    104–107
  default, automated, 229
  Facebook
    ads, 269–281
    plugins, 204–208
  Google Analytics, 169–183
  GTranslate, 210–215
  Other Comment Settings, 106
  SEO (search engine
    optimization), 150
  statistics, 161–168
  themes, 185–195
  widgets, modifying, 192,
    208–210
Settings area, navigating, 105
Settings link, 130
Settings page, accessing, 223
setup. *See also* formatting
  Blogger accounts, 22–35
  Gmail accounts, 21–22
Setup Checklist, 257
Share plugin, 215–217
sharing blogs on Facebook,
  32–35, 56–58, 215–217
Sign In to Your AdWords
  Account, 97
Sign Up button, 172
Sign Up link, 108
signups, Google Analytics, 172
Site Admin link, 53
site visits, accessing, 166.
  See also statistics
sizing images, 31, 62, 65
sliders, price, 109
Smart YouTube plugin, 231–234
social advertising, promoting
  with, 267–294
social media, promoting on,
  247–266. *See also* Facebook;
  Twitter
Social Networking Space, 204
software, open source, 221
spam, 101–102
  Akismet, 107–111

comments, 102
    modifying settings,
        104–107
    overview of, 103–104
    WP-reCAPTCHA plugin,
        237–241
    overview of, 102–104
special effects, 71, 75
Sponsored Stories, 285
Start Importing button, 249
starting. *See also* setup
    accounts, 41–50
    to blog, 27–29
    Blogger accounts, 22–23
    free blogs, 37–58
    hosting accounts, 84–87
Start My Free AdWords Trial
    Now button, 94
static pages, 195. *See also* pages
statistics, 161–168. *See also*
    Google, Analytics
    viewing, 168
status messages, 115
    BlogBooker, 119
storage, passwords, 44
strategies, promotion, 250
subcategories, 143
subdomains, 90
Submit button, 223
subscribing
    blogs, 250
    to email lists, 221–226
    feeds, adding, 262
support, WordPress, 38
switching themes, 185–195

T

Table of Contents, 146
    Blogger, 11
taglines, 131
tags
    adding, 229–230
    clouds, 307
targeting audiences, 272–274
templates
    Blogger, 26
    themes. *See* themes

testing
    subscribing, 226
    usability, 307
text
    images, 60
    pages. *See* pages
themes
    adding, 185–195
    Featured, 188
    installing, 125
    managing, 125
    News, 188
    pages. *See* pages
    paid services, 299
    selecting, 124–129
thumbnails, 78. *See also* images
titles, 24, 131. *See also* naming
    ads, 271
    editing, 230
    Facebook ads, 284
    formatting, 27
    images, 60
    modifying, 138
    pages, accessing, 200
    posts, 135
tools
    Akismet, 107–111
    Backup, 116
    BlogBooker, 118–121
    FeedBurner, 221
    plugins. *See* plugins
translating languages,
    GTranslate, 210–215
trends, 167. *See also* statistics
troubleshooting
    Facebook, 285
tutorials, AdWords, 293
Twitter, 7
    advertising, 292–294
    sharing on, 216

U

UIDs (user IDs), 171–174
uncategorized posts,
    categorizing, 146–147
Update Automatically
    button, 112

Update button, 66, 147, 201, 230
Update Options button,
    110, 234
updating WordPress, 111–112
Upload a Photo button, 74
uploading images, 60–67, 126
    to Facebook, 67–69
Upload link, 114
URLs (uniform resource
    locators)
    image links, 62
    search-engine-friendly,
        158–159
usability testing, 307
user IDs. *See* UIDs (user IDs)
usernames
    entering, 46
    prefilling, 43
    QuickInstall, 87, 90
    selecting, 41–42, 287

V

videos
    copying, 232
    manually embedding, 235
    posting, adding, 231–236
    YouTube, embedding,
        231–234
viewing
    blogs, 249
    pages, 200
    profiles, 178
    statistics, 168
    themes, 187
View Insights link, 289
View Page button, 254
View Page link, 197, 199
View Post link, 51, 137
View Report link, 178

W–X

Wall, Aaron, 153
websites
    fee-based blogs, 38
    nameservers, 86
    profiles, 172, 175, 178
    subdomains, 90

widgets, 12
Blogger, 11
Categories, 133–134, 196, 304
configuring, 224
Dashboard (WordPress),
enabling, 180–183
Enable Subscribe2
Widget, 223
Facebook plugins, 206
GTranslate, 214
modifying, 192
moving, 132
Search, 133
settings, modifying, 208–210
themes, 188. *See also* themes
Widgets area, 131

width, resizing images, 72
windows
Add an Image, 60–61
Add Images, 30
Add Media Files, 54
WordPress. *See also* **blogs**
Multi-User, 38–40
one-click installation,
83–100
QuickInstall, 87–92
support, 38
updating, 111–112
**WP e-Commerce plugin,
241–244**
**WP-reCAPTCHA plugin,
237–241**

**Write a Note
button, 254**
writing blogs, 27–29

Y–Z
**Yet Another Related Posts
plugin, 226–231**
you can get the keys here
message, 238
You may manage your
subscription options
message, 225
YouTube videos, adding, 231–234

zone preferences, 97

COURSE TECHNOLOGY
CENGAGE Learning
Professional • Technical • Reference

COURSE TECHNOLOGY PTR has numerous books that will help you maximize the job search process or excel in your current career. From creating the perfect résumé and acing the interview to developing the overall on-the-job skill set, we provide a comprehensive library of tools that will help you land the job of your dreams and work your way up the corporate ladder once you've got it.

101 SERIES

Create the perfect résumé. Ace the interview. Hone your skills. Books in the *101* series provide complete "get the job" advice from career experts for anyone seeking new employment. Tips are presented in an easy-to-read, pithy format, and each book is only $12.99 so getting the new job doesn't have to break the bank!

101 GREAT RÉSUMÉS
THIRD EDITION

1-59863-855-6 • $12.99 • 216 PGS

101 WAYS TO MAKE YOURSELF INDISPENSABLE AT WORK

1-4354-5432-4 • $12.99 • 208 PGS

101 SMART QUESTIONS TO ASK ON YOUR INTERVIEW
THIRD EDITION

1-59863-854-8 • $12.99 • 168 PGS

101 GREAT ANSWERS TO THE TOUGHEST INTERVIEW QUESTIONS SIXTH EDITION

1-59863-853-X • $12.99 • 200 PGS

90 DAYS TO SUCCESS SERIES

The first three months on the job are the most important! For those who have already landed the job and are eager to hit the ground running from Day 1, we provide the *90 Days to Success* series. These books provide expert advice and action plans for achievement from executives who have been in your shoes before and want to share their considerable experience.

90 DAYS TO SUCCESS AS A MANAGER

1-59863-865-3 • $19.99 • 232 PGS

90 DAYS TO SUCCESS AS A PROJECT MANAGER

1-59863-869-6 • $19.99 • 376 PGS

90 DAYS TO SUCCESS IN FUNDRAISING

1-59863-876-9 • $19.99 • 272 PGS

90 DAYS TO SUCCESS IN CONSULTING

1-4354-5442-1 • $19.99 • 336 PGS

90 DAYS TO SUCCESS IN GRANT WRITING

1-4354-5486-3 • $19.99 • 272 PGS

PERSPECTIVES™ SERIES

Ever wonder what your clients, customers, or employees *really* think of the job you're doing? Find out with the *Perspectives*™ series. In *Perspectives*, two or more successful executives share their opinions, but never collaborate, ensuring unbiased and unfiltered views of business topics such as increasing sales, building brands, marketing tactics, and managing employees. The frank "he said/she said" format of these books provides a unique learning experience as well as an entertaining read!

PERSPECTIVES ON INCREASING SALES

1-59863-874-2 • $29.99 • 311 PGS

PERSPECTIVES ON BRANDING

1-59863-872-6 • $29.99 • 276 PGS

PERSPECTIVES ON MANAGING EMPLOYEES

1-59863-873-4 • $29.99 • 300 PGS

PERSPECTIVES ON MARKETING

1-59863-871-8 • $29.99 • 377 PGS

TO ORDER, VISIT COURSEPTR.COM OR CALL 800.354.9706 TODAY!

COURSE TECHNOLOGY
CENGAGE Learning

Professional • Technical • Reference

CREATE YOUR OWN JOB SECURITY!

101 WAYS TO

Make Yourself Indispensable at Work

by CAROL A. SILVIS, M.ED.

It's now more important than ever for you to keep the job you have and make yourself invaluable to your organization. This hands-on, no-nonsense guide to making the most of your job, your performance, and your importance to your boss is filled with ways to secure your position and even advance in your career. The tips in this book are applicable at any job level and for any industry. Don't let yourself be the next casualty of the recession!

ISBN: 1-4354-5432-4
Suggested Retail Price: $12.99

Available at bookstores everywhere!

For more information visit us online at **www.courseptr.com**